T0162625

~COWBOY POETRY~

from a Short-horn Tenderfoot

Other books by Richard Bird Baker available through iUniverse include:

Letters From Across the Big Divide:
the ghost writings of Charles M. Russell

Corral Dust From Across the Big Divide:
more ghost writings of Charles M. Russell

New Spun Yarns From Across the Big Divide:
more ghost writings of Charles M. Russell

Afriats: understanding forced interpersonal interactions

Afriation Phobia: a psycho-phobic novel

COWBOY POETRY

from a Short-horn Tenderfoot

RICHARD BIRD BAKER

Sherry Gallagher, Cover Artist

COWBOY POETRY FROM A SHORT-HORN TENDERFOOT

Copyright © 2016 Richard Baker.
Author Credits: Richard Baker

All rights reserved. No part of this book may be used or reproduced by any means, graphic, electronic, or mechanical, including photocopying, recording, taping or by any information storage retrieval system without the written permission of the author except in the case of brief quotations embodied in critical articles and reviews.

iUniverse books may be ordered through booksellers or by contacting:

iUniverse
1663 Liberty Drive
Bloomington, IN 47403
www.iuniverse.com
1-800-Authors (1-800-288-4677)

Because of the dynamic nature of the Internet, any web addresses or links contained in this book may have changed since publication and may no longer be valid. The views expressed in this work are solely those of the author and do not necessarily reflect the views of the publisher, and the publisher hereby disclaims any responsibility for them.

Any people depicted in stock imagery provided by Thinkstock are models, and such images are being used for illustrative purposes only. Certain stock imagery © Thinkstock.

ISBN: 978-1-4917-9733-4 (sc)
ISBN: 978-1-4917-9734-1 (e)

Print information available on the last page.

iUniverse rev. date: 05/12/2016

Table of Contents

This book is dedicated to Liz Masterson, the songbird of the sage, a wonderful singer and recording artist and great model of a human being, whose courage and perseverance are unsurpassed. For years, she has organized and directed the best cowboy poetry gathering and western music festival I have ever attended, held every January in Arvada, Colorado.

Author's Introduction

No, I'll confess, I'm not a cowboy. But like most post-war kids growing up in Montana, I aspired to be one. The closer I grew to my maturity, the more I realized I could never be a cowboy because of my religion. What's my religion? I'm a devout coward. Cowboys, historically and presently, are real men, tougher than rawhide, gritty as fish eggs rolled in the sand, and bold as Blackfoot Indians. I'm what a true cowboy calls a stall-fed tenderfoot. That's a polite phrase for sissy.

Like many post-war sissies, I next aspired to be a writer. Kids with such silly aspirations were advised to attend college and major in English, which involved studying the works of the best writers in my native tongue. I "hung and rattled" until the college handed me a B. A. to get rid of me. I don't remember what falsehoods I must have told the faculty chairman, but somehow I bluffed my way into post-graduate studies for a year. My grades were so bad they gave me twenty-four hours to get out of town.

During the five years I academically studied great writers, I could never develop an appreciation for poetry. I wanted to write nothing but prose, both fiction and philosophy. Admittedly, I had a hard time understanding academic poetry. "Modern poetry" was academically "in," and like modern anything, I felt it was bland and monotonous. Meter and rhyme were considered too old fashioned and out of style by most graduate students and even most instructors. The modern "in" thing was called "imagery," and to this day, I'm not sure what in the devil that is.

I was the only grad student ever to achieve less than a B in a poetry writing class. My poems were branded "greeting-card rhymes," and the students with all the imagery and lack of rhyme and meter received the A's. One day, I asked the instructor why authors of non-rhyming, non-metered poetry always read their poems in such a monotone voice. She offered to award me a C in her class if I'd promise never to attend again. It was the easiest C I ever achieved (and one of the highest grades).

Over the years, I published five books, all of which were prose, but I never entertained the idea of writing poetry. As a performer of several types of traditional folk music, I developed a taste for pre-Twentieth-Century cowboy ballads, something virtually ignored by the media. The best places to gain exposure to this music during the late Twentieth Century were the cowboy poetry gatherings cropping up throughout the West. Hence, I came into contact with the only style of poetry I've ever enjoyed, cowboy poetry.

I soon learned most cowboy poets are aware their brand of poetry is deemed inferior by most writers, instructors, and enthusiasts of academic poetry. Perhaps that was one thing that drew me to the style. Two other elements drew me to it even more: first, most of it has traditional rhyme and meter, often in the style of our old-time western ballads that are so fun to sing. That makes the poems quite musical to the ear. Secondly, traditional cowboy lingo is so colorful in itself that a writer doesn't have to knock his brains out trying to hatch up enough imagery to offset the blandness of modern English. Nor does a reader have to scratch his head bald trying to understand a poem's meaning.

Traditional cowboy lingo, like the maritime vernacular of the sea, and even the old jargon of baseball, is so colorfully descriptive that contemporary, media-molded English is bland and trite by comparison. Often, a short, cowboy-styled phrase can convey more meaning and sentiment than several paragraphs of modern writ. That's the heart, soul, and backbone of cowboy poetry.

Many of these poems are simply intended to provoke a laugh or two. Others are intended to provoke serious consideration of a traditional cowboy value or sentiment fast vanishing under the landslide of modernization. As I am not a cowboy, and certainly no qualified critic of poetry, I don't know whether or not any of these poems are of merit. I don't know if some of the funny ones are too corny or simplistic, or if enough of the serious ones shoot true. It's my first rodeo to date. If you are not satisfied with the book, I'll refund your money, no shots fired. Chances are I gave it to you free anyway.

Lastly, let me offer an excuse for any faults you may perceive in these poems' meter. A couple friends who write "serious poetry" have advised me that in most styles of traditional poetry, the syllables in the poetic lines define the poem's meter, and by that standard, my lines break meter here and there. My excuse is this: most of the cowboy poetry I've read and heard doesn't conform to the practice of letting the syllables define the meter. Instead, there seems to be an imaginary beat behind the lines. Said beat defines the meter, the same as a beat defines the meter of our early American ballads. As in a song, syllables sometimes need to be stretched out or bob tailed to conform to that beat. In short, it might help to tap your foot as you read these poems. That's what I do when I read them at a cowboy poetry gathering. And if you encounter some commas that seem to have no grammatical basis, it's merely an attempt to introduce some pauses that clarify the meter.

Positive or negative, I welcome any reader's reactions to this collection. I can be notified by e mail at richardbakerbird@yahoo.com. Thanks for reading this collection.

This first poem is dedicated to Charlie Russell, the Cowboy Artist, from whom I borrowed some of these expressions and sentiments.

What's a True Cowboy?

Have you ever smelt a dally's smoke or felt the jerk of a tie?
Have you ever put your saddle in soak after losing your roll to dice?
Have you worked cattle who can't be handled by greenhorns or milk
maids,
Or gambled all night around a candle at the poker games we played?

Did you ever have to use a rope for more than a clothes line,
And burnt your fingers on a lope roping strays with that twine?
Did you grow enough hide over rope burns to cover a saddle or two?
Do you dally-welter your saddle-horn turns, or tie on tried and true?

Have you slept where the prairie was your floor and your only roof
was sky?
Did that roof leak, and through open doors, did the north wind
often fly?
Have you pushed hooves for weeks without licker, and each time it
started to rain,
Did you find you left your doggone slicker back in the wagon again?

Have you cooked on burning cow chips on a prairie without wood?
Tasted alkali on parched lips and smelled sagebrush where ya stood?
Did you ever rope a slick-ear, throw her down and tie her there,
And iron your brand upon her as you smelt that burning hair?

Did you saddle a snaky outlaw and ride for all you're worth?
Did you get back on, just like your Pa, each time you fell to earth?
Did you fall asleep on the ground at night to a coyote's lullabies,
And wake near a rattler first morning light, a lariat's length in size?

Did you flush them strays out of the draws and drive them to the herd,
Ridin' circle on a range outlaw, never missin' a single cuss word?
Have you listened in a bunkhouse to the yarns old punchers spin,
Settin' quiet as a hair louse, soakin' in their losses and wins?

Could you savvy what a cow says to her calf? Head off a charging steer?
Could you look him in the eyes and laugh, though his horns came mighty near?
Show me a man who packs just half of these manly ear marks and brands;
I'll say he's a cowboy, buy him a draft, and pump his shootin' hand.

There ain't many men left of that cut, grit and rawhide, 'cept their gun.
So don't feel troubled or in a rut, if I just said you ain't one.
There's more to being a true cowboy than settin' in a saddle,
Tony Lama's danglin' low, a big Stetson, but no cattle.

Today's young ropers and riders, who shine bright in rodeos,
Are cut from the same leather as the cowboys of long ago.
But born too late—the longhorns are gone and fences cut the range.
To see cowboys still holding on is a sight most folks find strange.
So let's not use our spurs until we cross the Big Divide,
To round up the Maker's herd where there's unplowed range to ride.

The Cowboy Way

Montana was wild as the long-horned cattle that grazed the open range.
The riders who herded beef from the saddle were too salty and gritty to change.
There wasn't much law when Montana was born, to hold down the lid
on wild folk.
And more than one cowhand tossing his horns, bucked out, as they say,
"in the smoke."

But a code of conduct settled the West, and the most honest place ya saw
Was Montana when it was at its best, before statehood and formal law.
Riding up on a ranch when no one's about, one could rustle what chuck
he wishes.
Don't pay for the grub; that's an insult; but cut some wood and wash your dishes.

Before settin' down at a table to eat, unbuckle your gun to hang up.
Snatch off your hat and unspur your feet, if ladies are there when
you sup.
Eating at a counter, wear your gun and hat, if they're in nobody's way.
Pour drinks to the brim—use your shootin' hand, 'cause that's the
cowboy way.

Riding up on a stranger, raise your hand to your hat and don't cuss.
Never look back at the rider you passed; that's a sure sign of distrust.
If you ride up on a man from the rear, or ride up on a stranger's camp,
Whoop a "hello" before you draw near, so he don't shoot out your lamp.

If you and another rider stop to jaw, dismount and let your cinches loose.
It'll cool the back of your snaky outlaw; always take care of your cayouse.
Never complain; it'll make you less welcome than a barkeep at Sunday school.
Stand up for what's right, do what must be done; when in doubt, mind
the golden rule.

Take pride in your work, be true to your brand, treat cattle like they're your own.
Keep up your sand; a cowardly man soon winds up afoot and alone.
Say it straight and plain, be fair but tough; shut up when there's no more to say.
Talk low, talk slow, never say too much, 'cause that's the cowboy way.

Never ask a cowboy about his past, or even his birth-given name.
Keep your hands above the table, cards close to your vest, in a poker game.
Never sell out a proven friend with words that cook his goose.
If an enemy accepts your bought drink, consider that an honored truce.

Forget you heard of the word "quit;" hang and rattle to stay.
You weren't born to kick, pout, or sit; that ain't the cowboy way.
Never ride a bucker too close to the herd or wear clothes shining bright.
Don't shoot a gun or shout angry words; you'll scatter every longhorn in sight.

Never touch a man's shooting iron, without his say-so permission.
Same holds true for a stranger's hoss, unless it's a fight you're wishin'.
Don't wake relief riders with touch—use words to get along thereafter.
And never dismount near a bedded herd; a stampede's a mighty disaster.

Close all gates when crossing fenced land; don't cut nobody's bob wires.
Pull out some staples to let your stock thru, and pound 'em back with
your pliers.
Never down liquor when working the herds; it's dangerous enough when
you're sober.
Keep your head clear and be steady in the saddle; drink when work's
done in October.

If a cow breaks from your end of the herd, fate falls to you to retrieve it.
When the trail boss says you will pay for lost meat, bet your hat you believe it.
When you're herding and branding steers, and rope up a maverick stray,
Burn it with the rightful outfit's brand, 'cause that's the cowboy way.

Never shoot at an unarmed man; warn every armed outlaw you shoot.
Ambush nobody unless you have fled, and they keep pursuing you.
Ride tall in the saddle, hang there and rattle, never let go of the reins.
When you get bucked off, get back on, 'cause that's the cowboy way.

Lucky Wheeler's Reputation

My handle's Lucky Wheeler, roper and bronc peeler.
I worked away my youth running cattle.
And never a bronc buster, line rider, or rustler
Sat taller or prouder in the saddle.

I blew in by chance from a Montana ranch,
Stone's throw from the Blackfoot reservation.
Hot-footin' I sped, staying three jumps ahead,
Of my newly-hatched, bad reputation.

This sour renown that trailed me to town
Can be sized up in a dozen short words:
"Don't rely on Lucky, no more than a tree,
He's lazy as forty fiddlers."

These unkind words I scarcely deserve.
My work ethic's nothing to doubt.
Gather round, boys, I'll unload ya some noise
Telling how my bad name came about.

This bobs up one day I was prowlin' for strays,
And the foreman rides up from a hollow.
"Take Lefty and finish the north forty fence.
She's a good half a mile to go.

"Load the wagon tub with blankets and grub,
Fence posts, bob-wire, and all tools.
Not till each post is grounded and the last staple's pounded
Should I see hide nor horn of you fools."

Three days twistin' augers and stretchin' wire,
We were forty rods shy of our goals.
Wouldn't you know it, from the buckboard we unloaded,
The last of Boss Knowles' fence poles.

"We're shy forty poles. Better tell Boss Knowles.
He'll need to buy forty to boot."
"When he hears that, he'll blow off his hat.
He's a back-archin', buckin' galoot.

"But if we could boast we cut forty new posts
From the fir-tree saplings upstream,
I'd bet my pinto hoss, doing that for the boss,
He'd buy us a fifth of Jim Beam."

With a saw and an ax, we pointed horse tracks
To the grove above the Missouri breaks.
On the rim rocks about, we spied all stretched out,
A hundred head of froze rattle snakes.

A rattler lays on rocks on spring days,
Absorbing the warmth they long miss.
When sunset begins, they slither to their dens,
'Cause it's cold as a mother-in-law's kiss.

Lefty gathered, "They was caught in a norther,
Trying to escape to their holes.
They're about six feet long, straight as wagon tongues,
And hard as your average fence poles."

"Lefty," I bark, "that idea shoots the mark!
What a work-saving blessing we found!
No sense cuttin' trees when there's reptiles for free.
Let's plant them for posts in the ground."

We each took a rope and built a big loop
And noosed it on a score of snakes,
Twining 'em to whence we'd left off on that fence
Just south of the Missouri breaks.

Pounding in the stakes that once had been snakes
Was easy as flipping corn bread.
I held 'em straight and sound, the rattles pointing down,
As Lefty sledge-hammered each head.

We stretched the wires tight and stapled them right;
Then we rustled and surrounded some chuck.
The time was about one, I guessed by the sun.
I declared, "Let's celebrate our luck.

"For days us fools have labored like mules.
I can't recall ever working so hard.
A short nap we've earned, before we return
With the buckboard to the wagon yard."

I'm libating jolly, dancing with Irish Molly,
My hooves trotting on a saloon floor.
I awake to Boss Knowles rapping on my soles
With the butt of his Colt Forty-four.

"I rode out to check on your work, and by heck,
You rounders are asleep in mid day.
After three or four days, there ain't one post in place.
You best straddle your saddles and stray."

As off he rides, we sit and rub eyes.
How could them false words make sense?
Thunderation! Can it be? Nowhere could we see
Hide, horn, or hoof of that fence!

The sun must have shined bright for a time
And thawed out them vipers, per chance.
And as we both slept, they slithered and crept
Away with our half mile of fence.

Montana Bill's Last Ride

It was years since I'd ridden, so I was rusty, of course,
But I swore I could iron the bumps out of that horse.
One pardner helped me mount him, another held the bridle
Till my feet was in the stirrups and I was square in the saddle.

I spurred him in the flanks and hollered, "Boys, let him go!"
He began to unwind, and that outlaw weren't slow.
He was snaky as lightning, a cyclone with the bridle off.
But I was stayin' in the middle without being tossed.

But then he kicked the lid off, giving me such a fling,
I went soarin' skyward, sure wishin' I had wings.
So much astronomy no man had ever seen
You may doubt my mind now, but my memory is keen.

I passed two dozen comets and circled forty stars.
I almost hit Jupiter and I took a squint at Mars.
I drank from the Big Dipper just before I started down,
And I turned forty flips before I busted the ground.

I lay still for a spell in total eclipse,
And I wakes to find myself in another fine fix.
My foot's stuck in the stirrup. I'm being drug to death.
Four hooves are tramplin' me; have I reached my last breath?

Folks, let me tell ya, I was saved just in time.
A store clerk unplugged that killer to head off his crime.
I says, "Ma'am, ya' saved my bacon; here's half a buck reward."
She says, "Here's two bits change. Now stay off that tin horse."

I picked up my Stetson and dusted my chaps
And hobbled to the door amidst snickers and laughs.
I've rode some tough trails as through life I've strove,
But I'll no more mount a bronc again than mount a red hot stove.

Don't Say Too Much

"Talk low, talk slow, and don't say too much."
  An old-time cowboy proverb.

Keep your eyes open and keep your mouth shut
If you want to live long; that's advice I'll put up.
The sun can't blister a tongue behind the teeth,
And soft words can't burn a tongue. That's my belief.

Keep your tongue corralled; let 'em size you up a fool.
Turn it loose, you'll prove you're a drop-out from school.
The mouth is the thing most often opened by mistake.
The biggest mouths look best when taking a break.

A loud mouth goes with a shallow mind, dumber than a hog.
Any sea man knows a boat's horn blows loudest in a fog.
Empty wagons rattle the loudest. Some folks are like baked fish.
If they'd kept mouths shut in water, they wouldn't be in a dish.

A whale wouldn't get speared if he didn't spout off in public.
Avoid saying things today that tomorrow get you licked.
The trouble with many folks is after telling all they know,
They keep right on a talkin', just to help the wind to blow.

Talk is such a sorry hoss to run in any race.
One can learn a whole lot more, with his ears in place.
When in Rome, let the Romans talk; answer slow and soft.
Like buttons on a fat man's coat, keep from popping off.

If use should wear out such things, a fellow's ears should last
Fifty years longer than his mouth that's working way too fast.
When wiser men are talking, let your ears perk up and hear,
'Cause hot words lead to cold slabs if shootin' irons are near.

The cattlemen I honored most were men of damn few words.
They understood and were understood; what they said was heard.
Open spaces don't breed chatter boxes out on the open range.
A word now and then in the northern wind is a welcome change.

But what's worse than the cuss who won't talk short and plain
Is the eyeballing rumor spreader, feedin' off his range,
Spreading sinful windies about every rider around.
You can't throw mud without stooping low and losing ground.

Telling such folks secrets is like using high-octane gas
To drown the flames consuming a haystack mighty fast.
Riding up on them's like finding a snake in your bedroll,
A skunk in the chuckwagon, or a turd in a punch bowl.

So say it plain, low and slow, without a sour note.
A sharp tongue, sooner or later, cuts its owner's throat.

Tex's Horse

Tex bowlegged to the table and said, "Excuse me, pards.
Before you deal the next hand, I want to cut the cards."
A card sharp snapped, "I've gambled in Vegas and down in New Orleans,
But a spectator wanting to cut the deck is a play I've never seen."

Tex no more heeded them words than a man who's hocked his ears.
He cut six face cards from that deck like a cowhand cuttin' steers.
He flung them face cards ceiling high; as they flittered toward the floor,
Tex plugged each card between the eyes with lead from a forty-four.

He shouts, "Do I have your attention?" the gun smoking in his hand.
"I've got some steer you need to hear and dang sure understand.
Some sidewinder rode off with my hoss; it was snubbed to the hitchin' post.
Of all the loyal steeds I've owned, I loved that gelding most.

"One day, this fate blew my way, in Texas, I admit,
And it jerked me to a low-down play no cowboy likes to commit.
I don't want to have to turn that trick I turned down Texas way.
What I did near trumped my life; I've paid for it till this day.

"I played the cards that I was dealt; they said I wasn't to blame.
If my horse ain't back when I finish my beer, I swear I'll do the same.
I don't want to have to re-ride that trail, so I'm warning you,
I better hear that gelding's nicker before my beer is through.

"I hate the thought of playing that card, but I will, let that be clear."
Tex holstered his gun, bellied up to the bar, and ordered a bucket of beer.
He surrounded that brew in an hour or two; then a cowhand pranced in
on a lope.
"Everything's fine, Tex, your horse is back, snubbed to that post with a rope.

"It was just a simple misdeal, Tex, nobody meant you harm.
The horse looks fresh as a daisy, and the saddle ain't even warm."
Tex flushed down his beer, stood up to leave, and bid us a merry day.
"I'm glad I didn't have to play the hand I was dealt down Texas way."

The barkeep bellowed, "Wait a sec, Tex," as he ambled to the door.
"Don't leave us chawin' at the bits to hear a few words more.
Don't keep us in dark eclipse before your yarn is through.
When your horse was mavericked in Texas, what'd you have to do?"

Tex spit his chaw in the spittoon and pulled his can from his pants.
Ashamed as a horse thief, he confessed, "I had to walk back to the ranch."

Two Dot, Montana

It wasn't Hank Sr., but his son, the greener,
The hippie/cowboy singer wannabe,
Who came to Montana in Stetson and bandana,
Barging headfirst into our society.

His welcome was overstayed in the bars we played
With his Nashville-star, know-it-all rap.
But one thing was keen about his years on our scene:
He put Two Dot, Montana on the map.

He recorded one song that just couldn't go wrong
In the voice of a bold Montana man.
Can't recall all the words, but the last line I heard,
Was, "I'm from Two Dot and I don't give a damn."

That song, a choice of both hippies and cowboys,
Echoed through every honky-tonk and bar.
And everybody heard the song's catchy words,
Saddled and cinched to electric guitars.

Through the amplifiers' blast, the dancing folks asked,
Where this place branded Two Dot is found.
The country folks wondered, how in the thunder
Was that odd handle hung on the town?

It was named for the man who ran the odd brand
Of two dots on all of his cattle.
Dots not close together, and I swear I've never
Seen a tougher brand to alter from my saddle.

Two Dot wasn't one for duding up none.
He was unkempt as a buffalo skinner.
His wife would explode and cross words unload
When he always came filthy to dinner.

"I'd be at a loss to find a cattle boss
More successful than you," she would hand him.
"I wish you had sense to take pride in your appearance,"
Were the words she'd use to reprimand him.

"Oh, it don't matter; that's just idle chatter,"
He always answered her plea.
"I know every one near, everybody around here,
And everybody around here knows me."

When in some place where no one knew his face
Like Fort Benton, Belt, or Great Falls,
He still wouldn't bathe, change cloths, comb, or shave
Before lining out to make calls.

When his wife complained, he'd tell her the same,
"Your idle chatter don't matter, my dear.
Nobody you see around here knows me,
And I sure don't know anyone here."

One time he hired four cowhands to ride
On a cattle train from Malta to Chicago.
Their job was to keep the cows on their feet,
Watered and fed for five days or so.

In Chicago one day, from half a block away,
The four cowpokes pointed Two Dot out
To two police patrolling the streets.
"That beggar keeps following us about."

Now as I remarked prior, Two Dot's attire,
Looked ragged as any sheepherder could be.
They took the bait fast, like a pair of lake bass,
And arrested him for vagrancy.

But the prank sure misfired for the hands Two Dot hired
When he coaxed the law into a bank.
The banker unfolded Two Dot had unloaded
Ten grand of cattle money before the prank.

The police then saw how they had been jobbed
And cut poor Two Dot Wilson loose.
They combed the whole town, turned it upside down,
To herd those four to the calaboose.

The four cowboy pards hid in the stock yards
Until darkness crept in and saved 'em.
Then they ducked in, to some watering holes again,
Spending most of the silver Two Dot paid 'em.

Meanwhile the two cops tipped Wilson off
As to who the slick pranksters might be.
His temper waxed shorter than a whore with a lead quarter.
He caught the next train back to cow country.

The four drunken gents had but eighty-four cents
Among the prank-happy quartet.
It didn't go to buy a bottle of wine.
It helped get them home, you can bet.

Three made it back, hoppin' trains to Bull Hook
And freight wagons through Judith Pass.
But one cowboy chose the easy way to go.
He allowed he'd just travel first class.

He asked all his pals to pack him up well
In a big, lopsided wooden crate.
With water, bread, and a chamber pot, it's said,
They C.O.D.ed him to Utica by freight.

They blew in a day before that boxed strayed
In from a trail long and tense.
The three passed the hat in each saloon they were at
For the freight's nine bucks and eighty cents.

These true words of grit ain't corral dust one bit.
Old-time punchers knew how to hustle.
The Kid in the crate found big fame in his state,
Later know by the handle Charlie Russell.

Remember Them Days

Remember when we used to ride on trails now plowed under?
And tried to hold a night herd spooked by wind, lightning, and thunder?
Remember how we had to sing to keep them cattle still?
How we'd round 'em up in early spring and brand 'em 7 L?

Remember we'd outspend drunk sailors each time we hit town?
We got to know the Sheriffs' jailers whenever they bedded us down.
If any wampum did survive, it went to the gals who'd mingle
With men spending half their lives as cowhands, alone and single.

Remember the days our bellies rubbed hard against our backbones?
We'd ride from ranch to ranch for grub; for a week we'd feel at home.
By the time the grub line was played out, and the last free meal was seen,
Spring roundup would soon come about, the cranky cook slinging our beans.

Remember we seized him, quite by force, and baptized him in the crick?
Next coffee he boiled was belly wash, his next biscuits hard as brick.
Remember the greeners we used to string with the snipe hunts we'd pull off?
Wasn't that the funniest damn thing; could make a sick cow laugh.

Remember the day your loop ya tossed 'round the neck of plump Mama Bear?
You lernt the hard way who was boss; you approach 'em now with care.
And the time I roped onto the horns of a yearling buffalo bull.
He snapped my twine like a stalk of corn after showing my horse how to pull.

Remember swimming longhorn cattle cross the Missouri's spring rise?
We hung our hardware on our saddles, case we had to swim for our lives.
Except that Texan, Nate McCall, the stubborn cuss who rode drag,
Plunged in sportin' two cap-and-balls, bigger than a hog's hind leg.

His hoss sank like an iron spike; then the hoss bobbed up alone.
Then branches, logs, stumps, and the like, fast into the river were thrown.
Hoping the Texan would bob up fast, maybe fetch onto some wood,
We held our lariats ready to cast, but alas, it did no good.

Then we saw his gasping head emerge across the stream.
He walked ashore, tall and proud; at last he was looking clean.
He stepped up that bank calm as a deacon stepping to a Sunday preachin'.
He caught his horse, swung himself on, and waited for us to reach him.

Remember the range boss starred him down, for a cold minute or two?
He wasn't a man to hint around; his words were short and few.
"When we unload a warning, we know what we're talking about."
"Boss, all that weight, held me down, so I could walk out."

Remember that rider Smoke Stack Lar? Couldn't he swing a noose?
He could rope any critter wrapped in hair and cut the varmint loose.
He'd rope the hind foot of a bear and the antlers of a moose.
They found his chopped hide, bones, and hair, behind the wheels of a caboose.

He'd downed mescal in a backstreet saloon, till he forgot the meaning of pain.
He'd waited in the saddle 'neath a dollar moon, to rope the stack of a train.
His loop fastened tight around that stack, but before he could dally loose,
That hoss was drug onto the track and sliced by the caboose.

Gritty men like that are almost gone; few today remain.
Most folks herd in noisy towns, where everything looks the same.
But the deeds we did, the stunts we pulled, and the range hosses we saddled
Hold out in the memories of old riders who trailed the longhorn cattle.

The Frozen Horse

How hot was it? Turn my way and lift your ears.
The hottest spell to rope and tie the Judith land in years.
The mercury in the thermometers all swelled and busted loose,
And every cow in Basin County gave evaporated moo juice.

The dogs still chased the cats at times, but found it none too fun.
The critters vowed as they played the game to always walk, don't run.
The chickens laid hard boiled eggs; I fried bacon on concrete.
The sun popped four acres of corn, in a field just up the street.

A rider tracked in from the east, passing through our two-trough town.
He'd ridden clean from North Dakota on his trail to Puget Sound.
His hoss was wetter than a carp, sweat foaming from the heat wave,
Like some barber had lathered it up, fixin' to give it a shave.

My Pa saddled up a fresh gelding, one we called White Herman,
Cleaner than a brand new mirror and dry as a Methodist sermon.
"Tell me," the NoDak* asked my Pa, "when riding in this heat,
However do you keep your hoss, so dry and clean and neat?"

Pa always thought of NoDaks as good but simple folk.
He always saw them as a shot at pulling a cowboy joke.
"What ya gotta do," Pa said, "when ridin' in this weather,
Is spur that cayuse in the flanks, and quirt it with some leather.

"Race it fast as it can lope till you're six miles from town.
The breeze the hoss fans with its speed will cool the critter down."
"I never thought of that before, but like a steer, I'll try."
He poured some leather into that steed and bid us a goodbye.

21

The mount scattered over hill and dale, sprinting for all it could muster,
And five miles west it hit the ground, deader than General Custer.
When that cavayo hit the dirt, the rider hit it too.
He bounced along for several rods, like a bag of bran would do.

He came to rest against a tree and lay in dark eclipse
Until a farmer lifted his head and put a canteen to his lips.
"Are you O.K.?" the farmer asked. "Looks like your horse went down."
The NoDak twisted to his feet, up off the burning ground.

He wobbled like a new-foaled colt till he could finally stand,
Searching himself for broken parts with the inside of his hands.
"Seems to me no bones is broke, though I'm skinned from head to toes."
"What cruel fate befell your horse?" "Poor critter must've froze."

* NoDak is Montana jargon for North Dakotan.

Con Price's Horse

'Twas in Cascade, just up the Missouri,
Where the Cowboy Artist was wed.
"No man can ride a hide packed with fury
Like twister Con Price," Charlie said.

A barber piped, "Set 'em up, Tony.
Put the round on my tab, of course.
Like I says, Con rides snaky broncs only,
So no thief can stick to his horse."

A blacksmith, a dozen drinks down the trail,
Says, "I ain't forgot how to ride.
When I was a colt, I was tough as a nail.
I could stick to any beast wrapped in hide.

"I'll bet ya my roll and my spurs or my kack—
Well, eight bucks is what I'll lay down—
That I can ride to the livery and back
On the first horse Con rides into town.

"It's the squarest wager I ever seen bet.
Charlie Russell here can hold the stakes."
The barber backs down with, "I can't quite yet.
I have four heads to sheer, oil, and rake."

The barber was still lacking, in the scenery,
When Con Price came bucking along.
We reckoned the blacksmith's eight-dollar ante
Was a wager the barber'd pass on.

When a dusty rider tips Con off
About the riding match he just missed,
He waxes game as a pack of wasps.
"Let's give this old blacksmith a twist.

"I allow he has an even break
To win out or lose on this deal.
I'll play every card I have to make
This bet come smooth off the reel."

Now why was Con chawin' at the bits
To see this saloon bet put down?
'Cuz whoever won, be it barber or smith,
Would no doubt buy us all rounds.

So he ambled in, his mane to trim,
To the barber shop early next day.
He assured the barber no man but him
In the middle of his broncs could stay.

One of his stallions had thrown a shoe,
So he repaired to the blacksmith's shop.
What he told the smith wasn't quite true.
The fib would be darn hard to top.

"Ridin' any of my broncs," he said,
"Is easier than men realize.
Keep a tight rein; don't give him his head,
And never spur them old hides."

The bet was made; the odds were lain;
The blacksmith was set to ride
To the Livery Stable and back again
Without soaring from that old hide.

Con pretended he hadn't heard
About the saloon bet, of course.
He faked surprise, then answered, "Sure,"
When the blacksmith borrowed his horse.

Three of us held the outlaw tight
And helped the smith get astraddle,
Till his feet was in the stirrups right
And his rump square in the saddle.

With one hand gripping the bridle straight
And one clutching the saddle horn,
He held that steed to a slow road gait
To the livery stable that morn.

He turned that killer horse around
And pointed him back again.
As he paced easy through the town,
It seemed the blacksmith would win.

But don't ya think it, for fate was bound
To lead that bet far amiss.
Herb Nelson, he's the village clown,
Was about to see to this.

Nelson wore a baggy canvas coat
When the blacksmith passed him by.
He shook it with a flapping jolt
Like eagles crossing the sky.

The outlaw bronco buried his head
And arched his back like a cat.
As into the atmosphere he sped,
Like a whip, he snapped his back.

He snapped the blacksmith Heaven's way
And it's many the time I've swore,
He saw more astronomy that day
Than any dozen men before.

He rounded Jupiter, nine comets he passed,
Took a squint at Saturn and Mars,
Chugged the Big Dipper like he owned the flask,
Just like the hooch in Montana bars.

He kept on riding this bad luck streak.
Once he heard his Master call.
When he fell back down in about a week,
'Twas a boulder that broke his fall.

For a time, he lay in a total eclipse
That blotted out his worldly views,
Till I held a canteen to his lips
And the barber yanked off his shoes.

"I lost my stake on that jinxed ride,
But there's one more bet I'll lay down.
I bet I thrash Herb Nelson's hide
When he next rides into town."

Big Sandy Lane

Big Sandy Lane, mule skinner, earned his keep hauling freight
From Benton to Helena or Bull Hook, in seven days or eight.
'Twas raining pitchforks on the day, this fate I now unfold,
Wet enough to bog a buzzard's shadow, let alone a wagon load.

He lined out for Fort Asinaboine with army grub and hard tack
To save the hungry soldiers' bellies from rubbin' against their backs.
He was running late by reason of mud clogging up his wheels,
But he kept on freighting, knowing how to best address his mules.

Them four mules were game as hornets to reach the fort that day.
Two feet of mud and a cascade of rain couldn't trump their play.
But then they reached a ragin' stream, swollen from spring thaw,
Tossin' and buckin' like a locoed bronc you'd call a bad outlaw.

They seen that stream arching its back and halted in their tracks.
No amount of cussin' could move that team; nor could the bullwhip's crack.
No prayin', shoutin', or chain rattlin' could start them mules either.
They was stuck on holdin' out until the Lord improved the weather.

Big Sandy lit in once again, doing what he best knew.
He cussed until the air within shootin' range turned blue.
He cussed till four acres of soaked grass sizzled like dry mush,
Till the cottonwoods shed their leaves, and even the devil blushed.

A flock of geese had their feathers singed off as overhead they honks.
Every critter within cussin' range quit the land like runaway broncs.
He cussed until the ragin' stream turned dry as a tinderbox.
He popped his whip, rattled some chains, and the mules rattled their hocks.

He reached the fort an hour after sunset tried to begin,
Just in time to keep them starvin' troops from cashin' in.
Now every fall that stream sinks where the wagon crossed that day,
And it surfaces again to the right, about a stone's throw away.

Some folks say that for corral dust, ain't this tale a dandy?
It's true as preaching; the crick and town were both branded Big Sandy.

Lawyers and Horse Thieves

He looked pudgy and weak, not a cowboy's physique,
Waddling into the bar called The Pacer.
"A gin and a scotch, put 'em both on the rocks,
And pour some dark porter for a chaser."
He was quiet to begin, then the tongue oil kicked in,
Causing his thoughts to cut loose.
The long row of fools on the long row of stools
Drank in his words with joy juice.

He spouted, "Barkeep, my thinking ain't deep.
I'm as dumb as I was back in school.
When the Lord dealt our cards, aces fell to my pards;
I was dealt a worse hand than a mule.
But one thing I know, from this valley of woe,
Is lawyers are lousy horse thieves."
He surrounded some beer, burped out some air,
And wiped off some foam with his sleeves.

A stranger on a stool stood up and he ruled,
"I'll shoot you this, dang quick and cold.
I corralled every word; I resent what I heard.
You can't slander my profession so bold.
I should resort, to taking you to court.
I'd win all you hold plus your hide.
Or if you're a man, we can settle by hand,
If you care to take this outside."

"Hobble your rage; don't rattle his cage,"
The barkeep advised the sore fellow.
"Surely you hear that he talks through his rear,
Shooting blank cartridges as he bellows.
Before his last beer, he'll insult every man here.
The teacher, the preacher, the fire chief.
You're a lawyer, I surmise, seeing your dander rise."
"Hell, No!" yelled the stranger, "I'm a horse thief."

Bronc Riders, Past and Present

Cowboy novels and B westerns
Dealt a lot of silly misdeals.
Such as: all cowboys were bronc busters
From their hats down to their heels.

That's a long ride from being quite true,
Even for young riders fit as a fiddle.
For not one cowboy in a dozen or two
On a folded bronc could stay in the middle.

It seems bronc fighters were born, not made,
And stove up well before twenty-nine.
It's said bronc taming, little as it paid,
Took a heavy butt and a light mind.

That empty-mind myth I'm about to kill;
The naked truth I'm fixing to unravel.
There's a lot more to getting spilled
Than being unloaded and tasting gravel.

Ya gotta know, one or two jumps ahead,
Just when it is you'll be tossed,
So's to kick free of the stirrups instead
Of being drug to death by that hoss.

Ya gotta fall right; there's no time to pray,
When you're soaring through sky like a rocket.
Grow limp; hit the dirt rolling away,
Before that killer sticks a hoof in your pocket.

Many an old-timer has said with a smile,
While watching a modern rodeo,
"We could beat these kids by a Mormon mile
At bustin' wild range broncs we rode."

But an old-time cowboy's just lacking sense
If he thinks today's cowboys can't ride.
They pack more guts than you can hang on a fence
And wear skin tougher than rawhide.

They're grittier than fish eggs rolled in sand
To take cards in the rodeo game,
Great as past riders of the frontier land,
And cut from leather that's the same.

Today's grain-fed buckers with a paunch full of oats,
Bred for rodeos to be living lightning,
Must be stronger than the grass-bellies we rode,
And even more disposed to fighting.

Cinch a buckin' strap 'round the killer's kidneys,
One that annoys the bronc's hide,
Few old-timers could've stayed in their Sam Stack trees
For the long, long eight seconds ride.

Any old-timer who stayed in the saddle
On a rodeo bronc, bred to unwind,
Would have to practice years for the battle,
Like the best contest riders you find.

But there's a full wagonload of difference
Between bronc riders of then and today.
And a man would just show his ignorance,
To say they all rode the same way.

Rodeo riders want them broncs to explode
So the judges can score high points.
Old-timers had to *calm* the cyclones they rode
To save themselves pain in the joints.

They rode them killers down to a whisper,
Taming them for working range cattle.
They stayed in the middle till their butts blistered.
That's what we called, "hang and rattle."

But the handle "bronc buster" is a false brand.
The only thing the rider might bust
Is his own arm, leg, wrist, or hand
When he mounts a snaky, ornery cuss.

Breaking a bronc don't mean killing his spirit
By slamming the young hoss around.
The end result—and you'd better fear it—
Is a spoiled hoss, unfit to mount.

A spoilt hoss is about useless as
A four-card flush on any range.
A hoss spoiler wouldn't last as long as
A pint of whiskey at a poker game.

Contest riders mount in a narrow chute
Where the broncs have handlers holdin' 'em.
Rodeo riders have pick-up men to boot,
To keep them broncs from unloadin' 'em.

Old-timers had to rope broncs in corrals
And steady 'em, saddle 'em, and mount.
They had to do it all by themselves;
On no horse handlers could they count.

Old timers had to stay in the middle
Till they got gravel in their hide,
Get up, brush off, and cuss just a little,
Rope the bronc, climb up, and re-ride.

Old timers used old rim-fire saddles,
A straight-forked kack with a short horn.
Known for their slow-sloped back cantles,
Most of them were old and worn.

Modern riders use a swell-forked saddle
With a steep cantle and high horn.
That sorta helps a rider hang and rattle
When the hoss wants to see him air borne.

Put modern riders on a rim fire rig
When an outlaw kicks off the lid,
He likely wouldn't win out as big
As the old-time bronc riders did.

Modern riders are tough as horseshoes;
All their feats call for real men.
But let's lift a pint to the old-timers, too,
Who blazed the hard trail for them.

The Texas Bragger

He was blowin' hot air at a Montana fair
When we first laid eyes on the tourist.
We heard him relate, "I'm from the Lone Star State,
And for loyalty to Texas, I'm a purist."

Just then my wife, the light of my life,
Said, "Allow us to show you Great Falls.
There's much here to see; folks here are friendly,
And they'll lend a kind hand when need calls."

Twelve miles over land, we reached Ryan Dam,
And the falls that greeted Lewis and Clark.
Their journals did say that from twenty miles away,
They could hear that falls clear as a lark.

"Do you call that a falls, those weeping little walls?"
Said the Texan as I admired nature's power.
"I had a whiskey vat that leaked worse than that.
I patched it in a quarter hour."

The next ride we took was to Falls Overlook
To show him the canyon below.
On a warm summer night, when the moon's shining bright,
It's so romantic—even if you're alone.

"You call this a canyon?" the Texan's mouth spun.
"This view is not so adorning.
My sidewalk had a crack much bigger than that.
I fixed it in less than one morning."

We showed him a trace of Malmstrom Air Force base,
Well known for its missiles and jets.
I said, "Eight thousand men are stationed within.
It's a vital compound, you can bet."

"Only eight thousand men?" jeered the Texan again,
"That don't hold openers with me.
I bunk more riders, ropers, and bronc fighters,
In one bunkhouse in the Brazos Valley."

Our last little thrill was showing him Smelter Hill
And the smokestack that towers to the sky.
The biggest chimney in the world's there to see.
It's almost six hundred feet high.

"It's not half as big as a Texas oil rig.
My outhouse for size far exceeds it."
I kept my lips tight, not wanting to fight,
But I thought, "This bluff peddler sure needs it."

"A man can easily brag himself out of a place to lean against the bar."
An old-time cowboy proverb.

A Wake for Rimrock Jake

Rimrock Jake, he was a corpse, though he didn't earn that title.
He emerged as such in no cowboy way; he gained it being idle.
I wish I could say Jake was horned by a big steer on the peck,
Or his horse stepped in a gopher hole, and the fall broke Jake's neck.

I'd like to boast he was shot from the saddle by an outlaw he was stalkin',
Or he trailed out from a snakebite while a lame hoss he was walkin',
Or a stampede drove his horse and him over a bank too steep.
But the barefoot truth is he cashed in his chips while he's asleep.

There's songs that say most cowboys lie beneath the prairie soil.
But Jake deserved a better send-off, one that's accordin' to Hoyle.
What's the best way to praise a rider who the grim reaper did take?
Waddie McCord, raised in Virginy, put up, "Let's throw a wake!"

To those who don't know a wake from a snake, McCord took to unfold:
It means settin' up all night with a corpse, a past-time centuries old.
He says long ago in Belfast, the strange custom began.
It spread like knapweed from coast to coast, all over Ireland.

In case the body was four-flushing, just faking to be dead—
Today I think the words "catatonic state" is how it's said—
Folks took turns watching said deceased, for a breath, a twitch, or a smile.
If they saw such signs of any life, they'd put off diggin' awhile.

Of course, if no one liked the cuss, they might not watch too close,
Not minding if they missed a twitching lip or wiggling nose.
Now a corpse, as a companion, ain't easily enjoyed.
Folks soon found it easier if a few drinks were employed.

It became the habit more and more, drinking to improve the stay,
Until the Irish Wake evolved into the debauch it is today.
Jake's funeral fetched loose in the Emerald Hall, two drinks after lunch.
The rites were over in half an hour; more drinks were poured for the bunch.

Word must've spread Irish whiskey'd abound, instead of rot-gut from town.
Cowhands blew in that Jake never knew, smooth scotch and bourbon to
surround.
Joy held the top hand; drink drowned the gloom; a band played polkas
so frisky.
But luck turned south just before midnight; the mourners ran out of whiskey.

A rider called out, "Don't put the lid on this mournful wake so soon.
Seems fit for us to resume these libations down at Con People's Saloon!"
Another rider put up, "What about the corpse? Leaving him alone would
be wrong."
They pondered that one till a waddie stacked in, "Can't we just bring
him along?"

Nobody anted up a reason why not, and as Jake was long and thin,
They flopped his arms over the shoulders of two cowboys, Wally and Jim.
Nobody sized Jake up as a corpse while his toes were drug through the street,
Just a cowboy who'd surrounded too much hooch to stand up on his feet.

Old-time saloons didn't have bar stools, just a brass-rail foot rest.
They lifted Jake's foot up on the rail, and propped him up their best.
"A bottle of rot gut and three tall glasses!" quickly orders Jim.
He pours a glass for both Wally and Jake, and another glass for him.

He dumps one down the cadaver's throat to help him come alive.
This play repeats itself four times, or maybe it was five.
"Say, can you two saddle tramps round up the sand to try
Shootin' a game of eight ball against me and Dan McBride?

We'll wager two days pay, or bet you every splinter we own."
The stranger sure put up said bet in a most cocky tone.
Such slams against their talents made them madder than a mink.
They couldn't pass a bet like that, no more than a free drink.

They left Jake propped against the bar, straight as they were able,
Snatched two cues and bow-legged over to the billiard table.
Wally said, "Get your money out, and get ready to lose it.
Eight-ball, billiards, slop, or splits, you two losers choose it."

They won the first game, aces up; then they lost the second.
The third was already out of the chute; they'd probably win, they
reckoned.
The corpse it slumps just like a man who's ten drinks down the trail,
Till its head and shoulders slide to the bar and its knees sink to the rail.

"You can't pass out in this saloon! Cowboy, trot along!"
Were the words the barkeep barked; the corpse failed to respond.
It's kinda rude for a corpse, I s'pose, to plum refuse to relate.
"I'll warn ya cowboy, one last time. Ya better pull your freight!"

The barkeep was big as a wagon of hay and stronger than a bull.
He was known for giving scores of saddle tramps the old heave-ho.
Convinced that Jake was a little rude for giving no reply,
He grabs Jake's collar and the seat of his pants and lets the drunk corpse fly.

Jim and Wally looked up from their game to see what had cut loose,
And saw Jake fly through the swinging doors, soaring like a goose.
They chased him out into the dust and yanked him to his feet
And drug him back into the saloon, the barkeep's snarl to greet.

"Now you've done it, Blackjack!" Jim puts up in a shout.
"Done what?" the barkeeps shoots back. "What are you talking about?"
"You got too rough with that old cuss. You done blew out his lamp."
"Can't be," the barkeep ups him. "I barely tossed the tramp."

"You tossed him across the big divide. Try and feel his pulse."
The barkeep takes hold of Jake's wrist, hoping these words are false.
But stone walls and steel bars provide a bigger throb.
"You shipped him to the realms of light," says Jim, "and did a good job.

"His heart ain't beatin'; he sure ain't breathin'; he's turning cold as a snake.
Wally, you go fetch the law, and I'll shuffle up a wake."
"Please," begs Blackjack, "You know I didn't mean to turn this card.
I'll tell you what I'll do, Jim, for you and for your pard.

"Tote him home, put him to bed, then say he died asleep.
I'll make it all worthwhile; that's a promise I'll sure keep."
"How worthwhile?" Wally raised him "How generous will you be?"
"Whenever you two track into here, your drinks are all on me."

"We need two quarts, to help watch the corpse," Wally upped the bet.
"Take 'em," Blackjack called his hand. "Here's the best scotch I've sold yet."
"There's one more thing," Jim ups him again, "Swear you'll never toss
Another cowboy out into the street, whatever be the cause."

"I swear to it," were the last words they heard the barkeep pout.
They slung the dead arms over their shoulders and packed the
cadaver out.
They drug Rimrock back to the hall and lay him in his coffin,
And surrounded scotch the rest of the night, checking Jake every so often.

They hoped when the corpse sobered up, he'd cowboy up in style.
But that card wasn't in the deck; he lay cold as a banker's smile.
Jake was planted two days later; a stone in the bone yard
read, "Rimrock died a second time to quench the thirst of his pards."

The North Dakota Bet

He left his pickup at the general store
Where he'd just bought all he'd need:
Dungarees, socks, and grub by the score,
Fertilizer, tool handles, and seed.

Then the NoDak farmer trailed in
To The Gin Mill for one cold beer.
An Indian eyed him with a fox-like grin
And said, "Hayseed, come over here.

"I have a quick question to put to you.
It's easier than you think.
If you can cough up the answer that's true,
I'll proudly buy you a drink.

"But if you can't answer this simple riddle
Let's say you buy my next one."
"Shoot," said the farmer, "I'll play a little.
Sounds like forty acres of fun."

"Who is the person I'm thinking about
Who's the child of my father and mother?
I'll give you a hint to help you out:
Ain't my sister; ain't my brother."

The NoDak puzzled till his brain near melt,
And his face turned sweaty and red.
"Toughest conundrum I've ever been dealt.
I give up," at last he said.

"I've heard you NoDaks are right honest folks,
But for horse sense you're lacking as a tree.
The answer is right there in front of your nose.
The person I asked of is me."

"I'll be a coyote," the stunned farmer flared.
"I'd never have guessed it was you."
"Here's how it stacks up," the Indian declared.
"In a second you'll see how it's true.

"I'm the second son of my father and mother.
Any bat can see I ain't my sister.
And never in my life have I favored my brother,
No more than you favor a bronc twister."

The farmer bought 'em both a beer,
Then called for a second round.
Then he pointed his pickup east of here
And sputtered out of our town.

Across the line he parked his truck
At the first saloon he found,
Itchin' to try that riddle's luck
On the first NoDak around.

There was nobody in that watering hole
But the barkeep and the flies.
And before I resume this tale of woe,
I'll unfold some steer that ain't lies.

Never swat them flies, if the Badlands you cross.
Don't spit out discouraging words.
It's a hangin' offense, by Dakota laws,
To insult or kill their state bird.

"Barkeep, I have a quick question for you.
It's easier than you think.
If you can cough up the answer that's true,
I'll proudly buy you a drink.

"But if you can't answer this simple riddle,
Let's say you buy my first one."
"Shoot," said the barkeep, "I'll play a little.
Sounds like forty jiggers of fun."

"Who's the person I'm thinking about
Who's the child of my father and mother?
I'll give you a hint to help you out:
It ain't my sister or brother."

The barkeep puzzled till his brain near melt,
And his face turned sweaty and red.
"That's the toughest conundrum I've ever been dealt.
I give up," the bartender said.

"I've heard you barkeeps are a right honest kind
With less horse sense than a banana.
The answer is right across the state line.
It's that Indian I met in Montana."

Belle Starr

The year was '64, in the hell of civil war,
When Myra Belle Shirley eloped.
A maid of eighteen, pinto pretty and lean,
For the richer life she had hoped.

Handsome Cole Younger, a Quantrill gang member,
Left Myra Belle behind with a child.
She trailed back home and was corralled in a room
To keep her from running buck wild.

On a day in May, after a short home stay,
She was cut loose by Quantrill Jim Reed.
With twenty armed men, she trailed out again,
Leaving Mom with her baby to feed.

Belle's first wedding rites were an uncommon sight,
Being married high on horseback, they tell.
They spent some time engaged in deadly crime
And even rode with Jesse James a spell.

Reed lived by the gun, was shot dead on the run,
And left a pretty widow to claim.
The next man Belle wed, was a cattle man instead;
At roping and riding she won fame.

They say she could ride and stick to the hide
Of a wild bronc good as any man.
She'd rope and throw a steer, and notch its slick ear,
Slick and quick as any top hand.

Belle's known far and wide, not just for her ride,
But also for the fancy way she'd dress.
Her bright clothes and locks were a lesson to peacocks.
All the newspaper writers were impressed.

She'd nothing good to say of news men anyway.
She claimed they all sized her up wrong.
But it didn't matter much; her luck was as such
That her cowgirl life didn't last long.

Her husband Sam Starr had a weakness for cards
And a temper, they say, that would soar.
A heated, short dispute about cards in a boot
Left Sam face down on a sawdust floor.

Belle Starr didn't pout; she calmly lit out,
Clad in a ragged sheepherder's disguise,
Found the cheating liar, and with a .44 iron,
She planted a lead plum between his eyes.

Belle hot-footed down to a quiet Texas town,
Moved in and dressed like four queens.
Became a church hen, and the society men
Thought she'd be the wife of their dreams.

She was courted by a banker; strong did he hanker
To see himself marry lovely Belle.
They spent time together, though she would rather
Than be married to a banker, live in hell.

She slipped into his bank to pull this next prank,
Knowing he'd be alone a spell at work.
He showed her the vault—there he was at fault—
For she pulled a .45 from her skirt.

She aimed it at him saying, "Don't make a sound, Jim.
Now go pick up that empty money sack.
Fill it to the brim. I'm not joking, Jim.
Hurry up, before your clerk comes back.

"My dear, it's goodbye, but make no outcry.
Your very life depends on your silence.
Farewell, my buttercup; come see me if you're up
In the Indian Territories, per chance."

Thirty grand in the sack, she swung into her kack
And rode like a drunkard to a barn raisin'.
She spurred out of town, her hoss burning the ground,
Singing this chorus to all the men gazin':

Whoopie tye dee ay aye dee aye ee aye oh ee oh
Whoopie tye aye and a deedalee ay aye oh! *

* The syllables in italics are from the chorus of the old-time cowboy
song, "Belle Starr," also known as "Bucking Bronco."

The Texan's Bet

Every June brings dozens of Texans
Up the trail through our Montana town,
All lining out for grand Glacier Park,
To Alaska, or to Puget Sound.
I've jawed with scores of these Longhorns
In a saloon called the Double Tree.
Most every Texan that I shook paws with
Sounded nice as pie to me.

But one got my back up last year
When he bellied up to the bar,
Boastin' and braggin' about the big crops
In his state they call the Lone Star.
Talkin' about some cotton ball plants
That reach seventeen feet each fall.
Then the chip spreader let these words fly:
"I've a brother who's twelve feet tall."

"Now hold your horses," I called his hand,
"I'm a pretty gullible guy.
But did I just hear you boast to the house
That your brother stands twelve feet high?"
"I'm a bettin' fool," the Texan put up,
"And I'll lay down this century bill
That I can fetch my twelve-foot brother
From the saloon branded "Boot Hill.""

I'm not a gambling man myself,
And I'll lay you twenty to one
You'll never catch me makin' a bet,
But I couldn't pass up that one.
The barkeep staked me to a century note.
I slapped it down next to the other.
"Go fetch your twelve-foot sibling," I dared,
And he lit out to find his brother.

I called for a brew but before it was downed,
He tracked in with two six-foot men.
"That's my half brother and that's my half brother."
He took the holdings and lit out again.
Kind friends, never take another man's bet,
Despite what you hold in your coffer.
If he didn't know something you don't know yet,
He wouldn't be making the offer.

Born To Hang

Jim Miller didn't seem ornery or mean; who'd size him up a killer?
Went to church each Sunday, and cowhands counterbranded him
Deacon Miller.
Never smoked or swore, drank, gambled, or whored; his many friends
swear it's true.
How it befell he threw in with hell is a fate I'm unloading on you.

Small pox took his Ma, snake bite killed his Pa, when little Jim was only eight.
He farmed for Grampa and scrubbed for Gramma; a hard life with them
was his fate.
Knuckles, misuse, whippings, and abuse, faced Jimmy, though he did his best.
After all he could stand, with a pistol in hand, he laid the slave drivers to rest.

The sheriff soon came; the law dealt its game; the judge said the
deceased were too cruel.
He sent Jim to live with a sister who'd give him a feedbag and send him
to school.
Her husband worked the kid, like his Grampa did, and cuffed him for
every mistake.
When Sis told him, "Quit!" she also was hit; that's more than kid
brother could take.

Church began anew, and from the last pew, Jim rose and cat-footed to
his horse.
The three-mile ride at a quick, steady stride took Jim to his brother-in-
law's porch.
Asleep in a chair, John Coop didn't hear Jim cocking a Colt forty-four.
A deafening roar, hot lead through a bore, and John would slap his wife
no more.

Jim fogged it to church; in a pew he perched, just as the sermon
played out.
He stood for a prayer, then filed out of there, shaking hands all the
way out.
The congregation stood by Jim's tight alibi: he was in church at the time.
But Miller was sentenced to forty years pentence; his sister saw him flee
the crime.

His lawyer raised hell; a new trial befell; this time young Jim was cut loose.
Ya can't blame a kid for doing what he did to a skunk handing out such abuse.
Jim took a wife, learned the cowboy life, working Mennen Clemens'
range cattle.
Till a marshal gone bad killed Miller's wife's dad. Jim shot the snake out
of the saddle.

Jim drifted around New Mexico and found he could earn his keep
gambling in saloons.
He plodded his way into the Pecos one day in the hellish heat of late June.
He found Juan's Saloon, ambled into the barroom, downed water to wet
his dry throat.
And everyone inside wondered what he might hide; he was sporting a
heavy winter coat.

A bully named Hearne thought he could learn this stranger some
manners of the West.
He turned on Miller with eyes of a killer, saying, "That coat you sport
makes me sweat."
Jim looked at the face of each man in the place, dusty cowboys with
dung on their boots.
"You're stink makes me sick, otherwise I'd lick every one of you drunken
galoots."

Hearne started the fun, put his hand on his gun, and growled, "Take off that damn coat."

The muzzle of a Colt sprang from Jim's coat, bucked and reared up at Hearne's throat.

"Hell's Bells!" Hearne croaked, "It was only a joke," raising his hands square and true.

"In two minutes," said Jim, "you'll be too dead to skin, if you still darken my view."

Jim bought a round for the house and downed—more water—that's all he partook.

Sheriff Ben Frazier downed a shot and a chaser and gave Jim a suspicious look.

"If you're on the run in this hot Texas sun, why sport a coat heavy as a mule?"

"When guns are in play, it brings luck my way; the man who doubts me's a fool.

"An old friend of mine, Sheriff Bill Cline, for years policed the border lines.

Every rustler around wanted Bill gunned down; this coat saved his bacon many times.

With boots off he died, with courage and pride, after giving this lucky coat to me."

Frazier admired Jim's grit, his sand and his wit, and signed him on as deputy.

The first two years went smooth as calves' ears; they worked well together, no doubt.

But like autumn leaves in an October breeze, the two had quite a falling out.

No one truly knew how much was true, but this rumor cut loose from its rope:

Jim drove stolen cattle with tramps of the saddle to Mexico on a fast lope.

Con Gibson thought he'd sweeten the pot and tell Frazier a white lie or two.
"Sheriff," he said, "Miller wants you dead. Said, 'Throw in with me; I'll
pay you.'"
Fearing no danger, Frazier loaded his chamber, commenting, "I'll make
this brief."
He tracked Miller down on Corral Street in town and called him a
murdering thief.

Jim reached in his coat for the gun he'd tote, but the sheriff drew and
fired first.
Five slugs from the bore of that big forty-four left Jim on his back in the dirt.
"And here's one for Con," the sheriff went on, firing a last round at
Miller's chest.
"I sure don't reckon, folks will be frettin', your absence when you're laid
to rest."

Poor Jim was brought to the sawbones' cot; we unbuttoned his furry
black coat.
Six slugs were peeled off a cast iron shield; then a laugh peeled from
Miller's throat.
"It's like I said. I should be dead, but don't this big coat bring me luck?
Now if you don't mind, I'll leave you and find out how fast our sheriff
can duck."

Cock sure that Jim was dead enough for him, Frazier found a saloon and
downed gin.
With his back to the door, he crossed the sawdust floor, and said,
"Dealer, deal me in."
He kept up his sand as he picked up his hand, black aces backed with
black eights.
The opener was met, he bumped up the bet, then came a sharp turn of
his fate.

Jim slithered in with a twelve-gage and a grin; both barrels held hard slugs of lead.
A round through each bore left the sheriff on the floor, more or less missing his head.
Four Texas Rangers, no strangers to danger, corralled Miller in the state pen.
The trial took a month to be played out and done; the jury ruled it self defense.

Jim ran a waterin' hole, two years or so, till fate dealt the hand he was waitin'.
He became a deputy, making him feel free, to kill every man he'd been hatin'.
Some say he killed eleven, some say fifty-seven, the eight years he was law's right arm.
Bachelor sod busters, sheepherders, and rustlers, never thinking he did any harm.

Jim came to see how rich he could be if he'd quit the law and kill for bounty.
Word spread like fire of his gun for hire; Deacon Jim was known in each county.
Sheriff Pat Garrett, the same man, you bet, who once outgunned Billy the Kid,
Said the rings on his horns now numbered sixty four, so ranching is all that he did.

A rancher named Cox was shrewd as a fox, and tried to buy Pat Garrett's land.
Garrett couldn't be swayed, so Cox up and paid, Jim two grand to play out his hand.
He was paid more to even the score in some grudge up in Oklahoma City.
The law sniffed his track, and behind his back, pistol whipped Jim without pity.

Jim waited in jail with no chance of bail for his trial to come around,
But word quickly spread Jim shot fifty-one dead, to ears of vigilantes in town.
They heard Jim's cut loose and dodges the noose each time a trial is dealt.
"Let's be damn sure his murdering's cured, and his soul finds its sorry
way to hell."

Vigilantes busted in to the flimsy county pen and chaperoned Jim to a tree.
A quick trial was bluffed; one prayer was enough; we sung one hymn to
his memory.
But the last request from this honored guest of this necktie party was denied.
We thought it a joke when he asked for his coat to wear as we cinched
him up high.

"Then allow me to sing, before I must swing, a song I hatched up in my cell.
The last thing I'll do, if you allow me to, before Lucifer drags me to hell."
He sang loud and clear for the whole crowd to hear: "No bullets could
ever kill me.
I've often been shot, but I always outfought, every man who ever shot at me.

"So tie the noose tight; I want to die right. Remember these words that I sang.
I wasn't born to run or die from a gun. Deacon Jim was born to hang."

A Cowboy's Outfit

When the schoolmarm saw us riders, dismounted near the draw,
She parked just off the shoulder and ambled up for some jaw.
We smiled hello and tipped our hats, and she said pleasantly,
"I teach history in Medicine Hat, but I was raised in an eastern city.

"I've come to learn about this land and its colorful history.
There so much I don't understand and find a mystery.
The first thing that I'd like to ask, I'm curious to know,
Is why you wear those big-brimmed hats I've seen in picture shows?"

"Ma'am, it's more than just a hat," said Waddie Bill, a true source.
"Oft times we must use it to pack grain or water to a horse.
Tilt the brim into the wind or rain, or the sun that burns your neck.
Its form is fit for fanning flames or slapping a steer on the peck.

"If you're in a shootin' bee, ya' shoot the top of his crown.
It's an honor to have a hole or three in your lid when you hit town."
She nodded a thanks and then she asked, "With all due respect,
Why do you wear those handkerchiefs dangling from your neck?"

"They're handkerchiefs back east, I hear, but Ma'am, this is Montana.
They ain't for runny noses or tears; they serve as a bandanna.
When driving cattle during draughts, they're a friend we love and trust.
Ya hang one over your nose and mouth to keep out choking dust."

"And what about those baggy pants you wear of stiff, thick leather?
Are they part of your attire, per chance, to help you face bad weather?"
"When ropin' steers in thicket or brush, ma'am, these chaps are worn
To protect our legs and knees and such, from the burrs and thorns."

"And I see your heels sport jingly stars, like I've seen on T.V.
To show you how ignorant Easterners are, what can their purpose be?"
"These spurs, ma'am, make a hoss trot right, when he's lazy or feelin' mean.
Spur his flanks, just quick and light, and he'll wax obedient and keen."

"As a girl I learned of the Wild West at the cinema downtown.
Roy Rogers, John Wayne, and all the rest, whatever films rolled around.
And all these handsome stars of screen were clad in fancy boots.
You're the first buckaroos I've seen wearing black tennis shoes."

Highline Hank rolled him a smoke and struck a match on his chin.
"Ma'am, this may sound like a joke, but I swear it's true as sin.
The reason our boots we forsake for these silly rubber prancers,
Is so you tourists don't mistake us for them town line dancers."

The Fort Benton Hanging

Some folks are born to live forlorn; others are born to seek fame.
Some folks are born to sleep all morn; some work hard to stay in life's game.
Some folks are born to take life by the horns; they often go out with a bang.
Some folks are born to raise wheat or corn; others are born just to hang.

In August of '68, 'twas Bill Hyson's fate, to come amblin' along down
Front Street
As the vigilance crew rigged a scaffold anew where Front and Geraldine meet.
"Lend us a hand," called the foreman of our brand. "Sure," said Bill,
"whatcha riggin'?"
"A scaffold to stretch the neck of our ketch; today's hangin' should be a big un."

"I'd be proud to take cards with you and your pards, in this game so bold
and hearty.
And, by the way, you didn't say, who's guest of honor at this necktie party?"
"You'll see soon enough," came a voice loud and rough. "Ain't no time to
talk yet.
Our elected chairman with his loyal hangman will be here soon, you can bet.

"Bill, get that saw from my brother-in-law, and start cuttin' them boards
to size."
"Deal me in. I'm hot to begin, if I can watch the show as a prize."
Bill spit on his hands like a hard workin' man, after he rolled up his sleeves.
He took to sawin' like a hound takes to pawin', faster than we could believe.

"I never miss a chance to watch a man dance at the noose end of a *macate*.
I'm pleased as sin to have a look-in. Who'd you say's swingin' today?"
"Is the sawin' done? You'll see the fun, when the hangman rolls his game.
Now take some nails from one of them pails, and nail them boards to
that frame."

"It's been many weeks since I've had a peak at an outlaw hung up to dry. There's nothing to me so pretty to see as a pair of boots dangling high. Some laugh when they die; some cuss and some cry; some pray and some take to singin'.

"Watching's a pleasure, a sport I do treasure. Who did you say will be swingin'?"

"You'll soon enough see who on stage will be, playing the human fruit's role.

No time for chatter. Climb up that ladder, and nail down the gallow pole."
The pole nailed down, Bill dropped to the ground; the foreman trailed back on a lope.

"Your work ain't done. Climb to the top rung, and I'll toss you the end of this rope."

"Just as you say. I'd work all day, to watch you turn loose a good lynchin'."
He caught the end of the lariat and then, asked, "Who'd you say we'll be cinchin'?"

"No time for jaw. Take that rope in your paw; fasten it to the pole tight."
Bill ties it down, returns to the ground, saying, "Who's to suspend from this height?"

"Here comes the chairman, along with his hangman!" the foreman hollers to all.

Up stepped the chairman, a former union captain, looking stalwart, dignified, and tall.

"Is everything set? Is the scaffold rigged yet?" he asks ol' range boss Bill Cline.
"We've tested the noose and the trapdoor to boot; the whole shebang's workin' fine."

"Then bring up the felon to meet our fine hangman. It's time to even his score."

Three riders seized Bill, tied his hands still, and stood him on the trap door. They slid the noose 'round his neck, sorta loose, like they'd done to rustlers many times.

"Hynson," the boss read, voice heavy as lead, "you're hereby charged with three crimes.

"One count of stealing a rifle from Sam Peeling, valued at twenty-four bucks. One Count of robbin' seven furs from a wagon, valued at forty-two bucks. One of shootin' dormant, a man's Chinese servant, valued at three hundred, if I'm right. Any last words you might want heard, before we ship you to the realms of light?"

"I've one thing to say, before we part ways, and the rope ends my trail with a twang. I never was born to cry or to mourn. I'll die like a man born to hang." Too bad Bill couldn't view, the send-off that ensued. 'Twas good as any; none deny it. The kind of hangin' which comes off without a hitch; Bill cashed in bravely and quiet.

A Father in Law's Bet

I shuffled into that smoky dive by no choice of my own,
Sent there by my thoughtful wife to fetch her papa home.
I can ride any critter wrapped in hair, rope and tie the moon.
But the worst chore I hate to bear is coaxing drunks from a saloon.

"He's your father-in-law," my wife allowed. "By now he's seeing double.
We need to wrangle him home somehow, before he mixes into trouble."
He stood bellied up to the bar, when I caught his eye.
"Please come home," I said for a start. "Nope. Not till it's my turn to buy."

Then in through the swingin' doors slammed the toughest man you'll see.
Able to whoop ten men or more, tall and strong as a tree.
"I can whoop any man in the house!" he greeted us with a growl.
And every man sat still as mouse before this bull on the prowl.

"I've busted a wolf across my knee, hugged a grizzly till he cried.
I've roped a cougar out of a tree and spit in a rattlesnake's eye.
I eat men for breakfast, cooked or raw. I need ten to eat my fill.
If any man dares to deny my jaw, he'd better write his will."

I told the old coot he's needed at home, but he didn't give a hoot.
He pushed me aside, wiped his foam, and bow-legged up to the brute.
He said, "My friend, no man I've met would doubt these words you've told.
But I'd like to lay down a bet, if I may be so bold.

"I'll wager you a century note, if the money you don't lack,
I can wheel-barrow a cargo up the road, and you can't push it back."
"What fer a cargo will be inside your wheel barrow, Jack?"
"What cargo we push is for me to decide. I bet you can't push it back."

The bully fell silent for a spell, thinking to himself,
"Any fool can surely tell this codger's weak as an elf.
What could he wheel that I can't? Not bricks, lead, or iron flakes.
He pulled from his wallet two U. S. Grants. "Let the barkeep hold the stakes."

Pop bowlegged out to his rusty Dodge, wrestled a wheel barrow from
the bed,
And wheeled it to the door of the lodge, where the ornery bully said,
"If you're ready now to lose this bet, let this rodeo begin.
I ain't met a man as strong as me yet." Pop said, "You're the Cargo.
Hop in."

TIME WAS

Time was I could stick to the hide
Of a spinning bull for an eight-second ride,
Back when I was on the sunrise side
Of twenty-four winters or less.

Time was I could rattle the boards
Of all them honky-tonks' hardwood floors,
Slamming down shots till three or four,
Lean and handsone in western dress.

Time was I could stand my ground
Against the bully of any town.
They took to a hole when I knocked 'em down,
When I was still in my prime.

Time was I could hang and rattle
In the middle of a bronc without a saddle.
But that was before losing this battle
To a half century of fleeting time.

I could woo the ladies on my bay hoss.
I took no lip from any range boss.
I rambled a lot to gather no moss,
Back fifty-five or more years ago.

How I could ride—point, flank or drag.
I was a top hand at pulling a gag.
Lord knows I don't like to brag,
But at shooting straight, I wasn't slow.

I was no green hand at spinning rope tricks.
I could rope and tie a slick in eight point six.
But that was back in fifty-six,
A good six decades ago.

At riding circle I was good as any hand.
Any stray shorthorn wearing my outfit's brand
Would be caught in my loop and under my command.
That's how I earned much of my dough.

In county fair foot races I could outrun
Any fast man under the August sun.
But that was way back in fifty-one,
Before sixty-five years loped passed.

Now I haunt the arenas I once rodeoed.
I watch cowboys ride and some get throwed,
Thinkin', "Hang and rattle till you're too old.
Age will rope and throw you too fast."

Now the only dancing I do at all
Is down the hallway to a bathroom stall,
Holding the railing so I don't fall,
Tripping on my own clumsy feet.

And it ain't a lariat now days I whirl.
It's strands of my mustache I sit and twirl.
My old sweethearts no longer look like girls
When they help me crossing a street.

I've hung up my riggin' on a bunkhouse nail.
I've hung up my spurs 'cause my legs are frail.
I lost my prime somewhere back on life's trail.
I can't ride nothin' wilder than a wheelchair.

So I ride a cane now at a snail's pace.
No burnt boot is more wrinkled than my face.
I'm gray as a possum with a fifty inch waist
Like my wrinkle-horned pards everywhere.

Can I still fight? In truth, I'll say no.
If I boxed my shadow, I'd lose a T.K.O.
A new-born bunny could chase me down a hole
If my hind hooves were a bit more sound.

Can I still shoot, you must be wonderin'?
Maybe I could, if you'd hold up the gun.
Without your help, I'd be a lucky one
If I could even shoot the ground.

As a young waddie, I rambled a lot,
But the past decade, the farthest I've got
Is searching for the handle of my coffee pot
As I circle the cook stove around.

I never took lip from no man or his spouse.
But now the matron of this boarding house
Flaps me more lip than forty muley cows,
Since the grand kids moved me to town.

When the Maker sends a rider for me 'cross the divide
We'll cross the skyline, as double we ride.
And I'll warble this chorus, loud and with pride,
Words Ken Overcast once scratched down:

"Keep ridin', boy, live till you die,
But don't live to be too dang old.
You'll wind up over there, in that old rocking chair,
With no dreams and no cards to fold." *

* The italicized lines are from the chorus of a western song, "Too Dang Old," written by Ken Overcast, Montana rancher, published book author, and recorded western singer/song writer.

Claim Jumpers in the Cellar

It must've been my lazy kid
Who left the door open wide,
Just an old-fashioned cellar lid
That opened to the world outside.

That night a critter on the prowl
Snuck through the open door.
He sniffed it out from wall to wall,
Corner to corner, the whole dirt floor.

He sized up the cellar, dark and damp,
And it suited the furry feller.
He staked his claim and pitched his camp,
Just like he'd built that cellar.

Next morning at breakfast, up seeps a smell,
Stronger than a long-dead steer.
And every kid at the table could tell
What sorta critter lived near.

We called the animal shelter, you bet,
And related our heap of trouble.
"Can you find a home for our pet?
Please prance over on the double."

"Sorry, ma'am, we can't take any more
Lovely, cute skunks at this time.
We've more than we can find homes for.
No, I don't want them in mine.

"But I'll tell you what card to play.
Buy a day-old loaf of bread.
Make a trail of crumbs from the doorway
To the thicket beyond the shed.

"If you play in luck, the skunk might swallow
Every crumb sprinkled on the ground
And eat its way back to the hallow
Where its last camp was found."

She said thanks, and we played the card
Suggested by the animal feller.
By morn the crumbs were gone from the yard
And *two* skunks dwelt in the cellar.

The man at the dog pound answered our call,
Saying, "This calls for drastic measures.
Go down to the Sons of Norway Hall
And rope onto one of their treasures.

"Buy a bucket of that lutefisk gunk
And scatter it across the floor.
It's the only smell that repels skunks.
It's a stench even they can't ignore."

We took the animal gent's good steer
And spread lutefisk over the floor.
By morning time the coast was clear;
The skunks trailed back no more.

Ma called the animal shelter place
And thanked the helpful feller.
"Now can you tell us how to chase
The Norwegians from our cellar?"

The Cash-in of John Wesley Hardin

'Twas a hot day in June in the Acme Saloon, but only a few men were there,
Croockin' their elbows, paintin' their noses, hatchin' up rumors to share,
When the outlaw walked in. "John Wesley Hardin," whispered someone soft as a bird.
Quiet as cats, they sloshed on their hats, and leaked out without saying a word.

He wore two .44s as he crossed the sawdust floor, twenty–two notches carved on each.
He wore his guns low like a man who ain't slow, fittin' perfect to his arms' reach.
Left foot on the rail, he called for a pail of the hottest fire water in El Paso.
Then laid out five dice before the bartender's eyes, saying, "I'll roll ya, two bits a throw."

The bartender shook, rolled 'em and looked. Five sixes stared him in the face.
"It's my misdeal, Price. Them's my *loaded* dice. Any honest dice in this place?"
To the back storeroom, where Price kept his broom, he went looking for dice to shake,
As through the swingin' doors, and onto the floor, slithered John Selman, the snake.

He'd been seeking John Wesley, all day and yesterday, to settle some long-past wrong,
With only one thought for the man who he sought: "John Hardin has lived far too long."
Forty-four bold men had fought Wesley face on, and forty-four had emerged dead.
The only safe play, to win out that day, would be shootin' the back of his head.

That plan in tact, he crept behind Hardin's back, quiet as a cat in a church.
A .44 roared, to even some score, and John Hardin slid from his perch.
When the law trailed in, Selman stood with a grin, and he offered the lawman his paw.
"Shake hands with the man who ridded this land of its most feared outlaw.

"I called his bluff. He wasn't so tough, when he drew first to pump me with lead.
I trumped his try with a bullet through the eye that tore through the back of his head."
"No hand will I shake with a murdering snake who shoots a man from behind.
That bullet did fly through the skull and out the eye. A man who can't see that is blind."

He was jailed a while, then taken to trial. A jury was roped up and gathered.
A sawbones was told to come forth and unload what he learned sizing up the cadaver.
"I swear I can't tell if the deceased went to hell through his rear skull or through his eye.
It's a blind trail; my science has failed, but I'll say this for the man being tried:

"If he's telling no lie, and shot Hardin's eye, I'll say he's an excellent marksman.
But if instead, he shot John's rear head, I'll say he has excellent judgment."

Household Hogs

I wasn't the brightest kid in class
Back when I was a young pup,
When every year the teacher would ask
What we'd be when we grow up.

Most of the boys were sure they wanted
To play baseball, be cowboys or firemen.
I always stayed my hand, undaunted.
"I'll make my living by the pen."

To make your living by the pen,
You face some hard crossings and bogs.
I was bucked off time and time again
Until I reached my goal of raising hogs.

A man grows rather fond of his hogs.
They behold me as a true hero.
I bring 'em indoors to sleep with the dogs
When the mercury drops below zero.

"You ain't got the brains God gave a flea,"
Said my wife while pushing a broom.
"You should know it's unhealthy as can be
To pasture hogs in the living room."

"It ain't no danger keeping hogs in here.
There ain't no just cause to fret.
I've let hogs in the house for years,
And none have got sick from it yet."

"What about the stench," she shot back.
"What can we do to deter it?"
"I reckon after a week in our shack,
Them hogs will learn to endure it."

Bat Masterson's Batting Average

The sun had gone down in that cattle town. Shaking hooves on a honky-
tonk floor
With Bill Masterson, was a woman no one, had seen in Dodge City before.
In storms a rounder who'd been looking and found her, twirling
handsome Bill around.
He shouted, "You whore!" His .44 roared; her soul was eternity bound.

After shooting his wife, he reckoned Bill's life should be taken to even
the score.
Bill's speed next to none, with a .45 gun, he shoved the jealous party
from shore.
As the rounder fell, he couldn't aim well. His last shot fractured Bill's thigh.
For months he's in pain, has to limp with a cane, and can't even mount
up and ride.

The way the cards fell, Wyatt Erp heard tell, that Bill's no green hand
with a gun.
He remarks, "What I need is a brave deputy. Bill, I baptize you the one."
One summer night, by moon and star light, two wild rounders rode in.
Shooting, as they went, at the Lord's firmament, raisin' the devil of a din.

They saw Bill limp up, like a foot-sore pup, saying, "Let your artillery rest."
They laughed like loons to see a crippled buffoon with a lawman's star
on his chest.
"Can this be true? A lame duck like you, is trying to tame wild men?"
"I'll tell you why, us one-legged guys, like me make the best law men.

"A man with good legs, if scared, could run away, in fear of soon getting creased.
So if you're quite through, I'm arresting you two, for disturbing this cattle town's peace."
They laughed like catbirds; Bill muttered no words. He busted them where they were at.
Words seemed in vain. With his walking cane, he knocked them from under their hats.

A polecat rushed forward to help his downed pards, shootin' hand reaching for his Colt.
He'd barely cleared leather, when the cane came hither, and laid him flat with one jolt.
Talk spread like knapweed from people who seed and sprout rumors all over town.
"Did you see the way Erp's lame deputy was batting heads all around?

"Three ornery men tried to hang up his hide, and all three he quickly put down.
I've said it before and I'll say it once more, and remind you when I'm around.
It's a plain fact he's better with a bat than most of us are with a gun.
It'd fit him just fine, if he don't mind, to be counter-branded 'Bat Masterson.'"

Never again did his foes or friends, call Lawman Masterson, Bill.
The handle "Bat" fit like a hat, till the day he was planted on Boot Hill.
Time slipped by; the bones in his thigh, slowly healed and mended.
Before the time came he walked with no cane, three dozen craniums were dented.
The mayor and his crew were all relieved too, to see the leg well and alive.
Fewer men needed burying with the Marshall carrying nothing deadlier than a .45.

Aunt Betty's Burglar

Aunt Flo's still pretty as a diamond flush, though her ring count's eighty-two.
By now, she's outlived far more spouses than most pretty widows do.
"I've buried four husbands," she boasted loud to the new man she's been trapping.
What she forgot to tell him was that two were only napping.

Aunt Betty wasn't quite so lucky; she's never been hitched yet.
Well, I guess she was two-thirds married to a fellow she once met.
Two-thirds wed? How can that be? When the preacher entered the church,
She was there, but not the groom. He left her in the lurch.

Once she received an obscene phone call; with nasty words she was showered.
She said, "He used such filthy language, and he went on for three hours."
She was fondled once in a movie house by a man she'd never seen.
"If you don't remove your hands in three hours, I'm warning you, I'll scream."

One evening, Aunt Betty came home while a burglar was in the house.
He ducked under the old maid's bed and lay quiet as a louse.
She spotted his shoes and snatched a pistol from her dresser drawer.
She said, "Come out with your hands up," and looked him over twice or more.

Holding the pistol in one hand, she pushed 9-1-1 with the other.
"I'll teach you to mess around with a woman older than your mother."
She told the cops she corralled a burglar that eve so lonesome and boring.
"I want you to come take him to jail, first thing in the morning."

The thief begged, "Ma'am, please let me go; I ain't done nothing bad."
"You ain't too young or old to learn," were all the words she had.
She no longer has that queen-sized bed; she has twin beds instead.
She allows fate now lays twice the odds of a burglar under a bed.

Politically Correct Talk

From mud, God made a man called Adam, and soon he sculpted Eve.
They disobeyed God's firm command, so he told them to leave.
To help make their lives run smoother, so they don't take themselves too serious,
God endowed them with a sense of humor, so they wouldn't wax delirious.

It's good medicine to laugh at ourselves when we're dealt a hand of pain.
Any one who can turn that trick has a tight hold on life's reins.
We're the only critters who can laugh ('cept chimps and catbirds, I'm guessing).
Now folks with less humor than a calf want to bushwhack God's great blessing.

I recall when I was young and cocky, humor sat square in the saddle.
It took more than common-place bucking to toss it from the cantle.
Today folks get burrs under their saddle from any joke that ain't "nice,"
Touchy as a den of rattle snakes, thin-skinned as baby field mice.

Too quick on the trigger to bellow words I never heard in my youth:
"Harassment, sexist, ageist, racist, politically incorrect, and uncouth."
But nature's hung funny brands and earmarks on every breed of us.
Once folks could laugh at themselves, with no offense or fuss.

Now this flapdoodle called "politically correct" makes cowards of some folks,
Afraid they'll trigger off sour feelings with formerly funny jokes.
So let's pull the saddle off our resentment and rib each other once more.
Laughing at ourselves enriches our lives, even when we're old and poor.

But let me saw off a bit of steer to ponder for a while.
When you sling a joke at somebody near, say it with a smile.
God gave us humor to ease pain, not to cause a sour note.
A sharp tongue will, sooner or later, cut its owner's throat.

A Politically Uncorrect Joke

Montanans once could take a joke about our towns and kin,
Before politically correct folk had yet come barging in.
This recent fear of old-time wit has become a hoss on us.
Instead of laughing along with it, folks take to argue and fuss.

This plague ain't confined to the city, or the liberals on T.V.
It's mowed down humor without pity, most every place you see.
I was crookin' my elbow in the Halsinki Saloon, warming my tonsils as
needed,
When in blows some miner's grandson, and camped near where I was seated.

He ordered a scotch, pulled out his makings, and rolled himself a smoke.
He blew a smoke ring and said, "Barkeep, wanna hear a Polish joke?"
The barkeep arched his back up high, like a bronc fixin' to explode.
He lowered his horns and pawed the sod. "There's something you should
know.

"You can see I stand six foot four and weigh two forty-three.
I was a pro boxer who won thirty-four, and I'm Polish as can be.
Perched two stools away from you is a man who played pro ball.
He's six foot six, weighs two seventy-two, and he's Polish as he is tall.

"That lumberjack there's six foot seven and weighs two ninety-three.
He can bend a horseshoe with his bare hands, and he's more Polish than me.
Still want to tell your Polish joke?" he asked as he squeezed two limes.
The stranger lit another smoke. "Not if I have to explain it three times."

Politically Correct Cowboys

This politically correct talk we can't help overhear
Has been spreading like knapweed, afar and near.
Instead of calling a feller bald, like we used to say,
"He's in follicle regression," is what we hear today.

Instead of saying, "He's grown a beer gut," like we used to do,
"He's developed a liquid grain storage facility," now they'll tell you.
Instead of saying, "He's fallen-down drunk," like we said before,
"He's gotten inadvertently horizontal," is what we hear any more.

Instead of saying a man's stupid, though it might be true,
"He suffers from minimal cranial development," they'll say to you.
Instead of admitting, "We got lost," like we honestly do,
It's, "We discovered alternative destinations and routes to see us through."

Instead of saying, "The lady's quiet," a trait we'd surly value,
"She's a conversational minimalist," is what her friends now tell you.
Instead of calling you a "cradle robber" if you wed a younger gal,
"He prefers generationally differential relationships," are words I can't spell.

If we had a cowboy who was short, we'd dang sure call him that.
Now these politically correct folks say, "He's anatomically compact."
And if a fellow's a spoiled snob because his dad was rich,
"A recipient of parental asset infusion," they call the sonofabitch.

A kid who likes to soup up cars has a "vehicular addiction,"
And a guy with his head up his rump has "rectal cranial inversion."
"Physically combustible" is correct now days for a gal with a hot body.
I'm not a chauvinist pig no more; the term's "swine empathy."

Don't tell me I eat like a pig; I suffer from "reverse bulimia."
I don't shun commitment; I'm "monogamously challenged," I tell ya.
If I undress a woman with my eyes, them aint nice words to use.
Call it "an introspective pornographic moment," so you don't ignite my fuse.

Don't say I'm an awful dancer; say I'm "overly caucasion."
I ain't no woman chaser; I'm "of the romantically oriented persuasion."
And when I sing old cowboy songs, I no longer call steers dogies.
"Get along, little disenfranchised mobile nurture seekers" are the words
they told me.

The question that trails up now, when all is said and done,
Is, what politically correct brand on cowboys should be hung?
The handle "cowboys" was hung on us because it seemed to fit.
Most of us still *were* boys throwing in with our first outfit.

Today these young waddies, like human beings in the herd,
Wax touchy as teased rattlesnakes when you utter the wrong word.
Who wants to be called a "boy" these days, twenty years after you're born?
To be addressed with this diminutive can cause a rider to rattle his horns.

But there's other handles for us knights of the range; just take your pick.
If you call us "waddies" or "cowhands," no one's bound to kick.
"Bronc peelers" or "bronc twisters" are good titles, tough and raw,
To be used for only the best of riders who can break a snaky outlaw.

"Cowsharps" is a good handle too, for the most experienced hands.
But I'd say the proud word "cattleman," is our best earmark or brand.
That word sounds plum respectful, and much sweeter to my ear,
Than "two-legged ungulate over-persons" or "cattleurgical engineers."

The only brand I hate to hear is that rotten word "cowpoke."
To us old-timers, it's a slap in the face, even when used as a joke.
Don't confuse it with the word "cowpuncher," a word not of bad taste.
That handle's been around two centuries; came from Scotland or some place.

But the word "cowpoke" didn't bob up till fences cut the range.
Railroads replaced long cattle drives and a cowboy's life sure changed.
A "cowpoke" was a cowhand who kept cattle on their feet
By poking them in railroad cars, so as not to bruise the meat.

Dime novels and B movies called even good riders "cowpokes,"
Even if they never worked a train, and took up ranching, like most folks.
I'll tell ya why the word "cowpoke" was hated by riders I know.
We worked Texas longhorns, hot-blooded as their kin the buffalo.

Those outlaws didn't need no pokin', no more than a mad grizzly.
What they needed was calming down, so's not to start a stampede.
It took real men to handle them killers, men of leather, grit and sand.
Longhorns were damn near dangerous as the bison who roamed the land.

But now your beef is cut from cattle that look a lot like hogs,
With bodies big as a Murphy wagon and legs like weener dogs,
And horns too short to fight a rabbit; to nature, they're a joke.
That's why it ain't politically correct to call me a "cowpoke."

A Country Preacher

Papa was a country preacher who always let 'em know
When the road they chose to travel was the wrong row to hoe.
One day from the pulpit he said, "Dear friends and kin,
One man here courts damnation; he's on the path of sin.
May God have mercy on him, for I'll swear upon my life
He's committing adultery with a good church member's wife.
I want to help him save his soul without marring his fate.
I'll keep his secret if he puts a Ben Franklin in the plate."
I couldn't count when I passed the plate; I was still a young fool.
But I roped in a pile of hundreds big enough to burn a wet mule.

Another Sunday he told the flock, "I have some tidings to spread.
The first glad tiding rings with joy, but my second tiding rings sad.
The good news is we have the funds to build that new wing, thanks.
The bad news is that money's still in your pockets and your banks."
Then there's the sermon he took the pulpit and told the congregation,
"Alcohol's the biggest plague ever to curse our nation.
In my right hand I hold three worms, in my left a glass of gin.
What happens when I drop these worms in this drink of sin?"

The worms sloshed into the deadly gin and did what you would do.
They shriveled up dead as Julius Cesar in just a second or two.
"What can we learn from the worms' fate?" the preacher asked the crowd.
Before we could bat an eye or an ear, my Uncle George blows in loud.
Uncle George is different from his kin; workaholic's the brand to use.
Whenever he does a little work, it makes him want to drink booze.
He's been warned about the poison he drinks by every sawbones in town.
"If you won't quit drinking that deadly whiskey, dilute every shot you down."
He swore he would and to this day, and in all days to come,
Before George downs a glass of whiskey, he always dilutes it with rum.

One doc said, "Take only one drink per day for the rest of your life."
George swore to the doc, "Just one per day;" he even promised his wife.
George had just downed his daily drink for April thirty-third,
Followed by May first and second in the next year of Our Lord.
Then he bowlegged into my Pa's church in time to hear him ask,
"What do we learn from these dead worms about the gin in this glass?"
"We learned," bellows Uncle George, "that if we drink enough gin,
We won't be providing room and board to worms inside our skin."

One day Pa preached, "The Savior said, 'Love your enemies.'
If we do as He commands, from enemies we'll be free.
It takes a bale of courage to love those who do us wrong,
But likely they'll return that love some day before long.
Is there any one among us today who can testify to me
That they are truly living in peace, without an enemy?"
Uncle George raised a paw, and snorted one word, "Me."
Pa smiled on high, crossed himself, and whooped, "Well, Glory be!
Tell us, George, why you're so blessed to have no enemies?"
George raised his shoulders, crowing, "I outlived the damn horse thieves."

Gentleman Black Bart

Step up you rounders if you want to hear
Of the bandit no honest souls need fear.
On the eighteenth of July, 1875,
Nary a man is still alive
Who rode life's trails that exciting year.

The Milton stagecoach was stopped that day
By a man on foot, the passengers say,
Wearing a long linen duster and a flour sack.
A twelve gage scattergun's what he packed.
"Please throw down the Wells Fargo box, I pray."

A lady said, "Sir, take my purse,
But kindly make a promise first,
Not to harm a one of the travelers here.
They're all good people, kind and dear.
Fear for them causes my heart to burst."

"Keep your purse," he kindly commenced.
"Keep your money and jewels, friends.
The Wells Fargo shipment's all I desire.
So if your guard will hold his fire,
I'll bid good day to you ladies and gents."

That hold-up grossed a hundred sixty clams,
The first of twenty-eight by this courteous man.
No circuit preacher or tin horn gambler
Was more polite that this stray rambler
As his legend spread across the land.

Black Bart was also a cowboy poet,
And he decided everyone should know it.
In '77, at the scene of a hoist,
He left a little poem to voice
His spite for the rich. His last lines show it:

...I've labored long and hard for bread
For honor and for riches.
But on my corns too long you've tread
You fine-haired sons of bitches.
Let come what may, I'll try it on.
My condition can't be worse.
And if there's money in that box,
'Tis munny in my purse.
                    Black Bart, the PO8. *

Bart spent eight years on this hold-up spree
Until November Third, 1883.
He robbed the Milton stage in the dark,
But he dropped a hanky with his laundry mark
At the foot of a cottonwood tree.

Wells Fargo detectives trailed that clue
And corralled Bart in a week or two.
He was sentenced to prison for six years,
But was pardoned when pushing five, we hear,
And he vanished in a year or two.

Not a word about him was heard since then,
This most mysterious of highway men.
On foot this robber always appeared,
And on foot he always disappeared,
For he feared all horses till the end.

* The italicized lines are from the original poem Black Bart left at the scene in 1877.

I Could've Whooped That Feller

I'm no easy cuss to rile up, and fightin' can't be right.
Ever since I was a clumsy pup, I've declined cards in fights.
Today's the closest I've ever come to kissin' two lips with my fist,
'Cause when it comes to flingin' dung, his big mouth topped my list.

I was waiting for the light to change, headin' west on Second Street,
When a shot-gun rider from the nearest lane yelled from the passenger seat.
I was hoping to hear, "How's it grazing? Ain't seen ya in two moons."
But what he yelled was, "Can't you do something about those stinking fumes?"

I rope and throw steers, brand their rears, and never lose the fight.
I whittle their ears and drive them steers to a bed ground for the night.
I close-herd the ornery critters to the outfit's roundup pool.
I reckon a man who punches steers could punch a mouthy fool.

I could've whooped that feller, although he was bigger and younger.
And don't dare think I waxed yeller, but for fightin' I lost my hunger.
There's no sense getting arrested, and causing my wife more gloom,
Because a damn fool shoots his mouth off about my stinking fumes.

Men are sorta' like matches; when they flare, they lose their heads.
Stay in the middle, look straight ahead, and bridle your tongue instead.
Don't go wading in riled water just because of a jackass's talkin'.
So when that stop light turned to green, I just kept on walkin'.

Last Words Before Cashing In

The question I often hear let fly by modern city birds
Is: when an outlaw's hung up to dry, what are his last words?
These final spoken words sure vary, depending on time and place.
Some are cheerful, perk, and merry; others an earful of disgrace.

Seconds before Tom Horne was swung, he told the men of the law,
"You're the sickest lookin' bunch of sheriffs I ever saw."
Ed Yager of Henry Plummer's gang, who squealed on the rest,
When standing on the scaffold to hang, sure lived up to the test.

Ed congratulated the vigilantes as the noose slid over his neck.
"Goodbye boys. You all are dandies, with a good undertaking, by heck."
Clubfoot George Lane of Plummer's gang was fearless to the end.
He said as he was set to hang, "Goodbye, old fellow," to a friend.

Johnny Cooper of the Plummer gang took the affair as a joke.
His last words when he was swung off were, "Anybody got a smoke?"
Henry Plummer wasn't so bold; he couldn't calm his strife.
He wept and begged the posse, I'm told, to spare his wicked life.

Plummer's men Jack Gallagher, Boone Helms, and George Ives
Cussed out their executioners before they lost their lives.
Killer Jim Heath made this request when he was about to die:
"Promise not to shoot holes I my vest when you swing me high."

Hayes Lyons never did repent, but he made one last request.
He asked if his corpse could be sent back to his former mistress.
Bill Bunton was a funny chump with the last words he chose.
As he took the final jump, he yelled, "One, two, three, here goes!"

Alex Carter of Plummer's gang seemed like a quiet gent.
He was the only one to hang saying, "I'm innocent."
Cy Skinner broke loose on the run, wanting the crowd to shoot.
They roped and tied him down for fun, then hung the evil galoot.

When George Brown was fixing to die, he assumed a preacher's roll.
He turned his gaze up to the sky. "God Almighty, save my soul."
One killer's hangman was two minutes late—his name I didn't hear tell.
He barked, "Hurry up. I've got a date with the devil for lunch in hell!"

Cherokee Bill was an ornery man. Before they hung him high,
Said, "I didn't come here to wind jam. I came here for to die."
Big Steve Laramie killed too oft; he finally paid his dues.
He asked, "Before you swing me off, would you pull off my shoes?"

Dutch John of the Plummer gang had but a minute to live.
Shortly before he was to hang, said, "There's someone I hope will forgive."
He called for paper and pen and wrote his mother, sweet and nice,
"Forgive me for throwing in with men full of sin and avarice."

Texas outlaw Bill Langley gave a long sermon about sin,
Saying he'd forgiven everybody, as our Lord had forgiven him.
He asked the crowd to forgive his crimes, and then he asked his friends,
"Don't avenge my death this time; I deserve to meet my end."

Other bandits were shot down while a stage or train a robbin'.
Sam Bass' last words were, "Let me go! The world around me's bobbin'."
Doc Holiday died from his T.B. He tried long not to show it.
His last words were, "This is funny. I expected to die from a bullet."

Johnny Ringo's final whispers for the law to hear
Was, "Please don't tell my sisters about my outlaw career."
Marshall Ed Short shot Charlie Bryant, an outlaw on the roam.
"Please pull my boots off peaceful and quiet. Don't tell the folks back home."

George Black was shot up by a posse after he robbed a train.
The dying words, "Pull my boots off," were heard by the law again.
When Wyatt Earp shot Billy Clayton, the same request cut loose.
"I promised my mother I'd never cash in wearing soiled boots."

...So go write a letter to my dear grey-haired mother.
Please do the same for my sister so dear.
But please not a word of all this should you utter
If someone should ask for my story to hear.

Get six Jolly cowboys to carry my coffin,
Six pretty maidens to sing me a song.
Put bunches of roses on top of my casket,
Roses to soften the clods as they fall.

Go beat the drums slowly as play the fife lowly.
Play the death march as you carry me along.
Take me to the green valley and lay the sod o'r me
For I'm a young cowboy who surely done wrong. *

* From the traditional Texas cowboy song, "Cowboy's Lament,"
also known as "The Streets of Laredo."

A NoDak Fishing Trip

'Twas sunset that day in the sweet month of May
When the NoDaks reeled in their fourth fish.
As they rowed to the dock near Holter Lake Rock
The two sad men abandoned their wish.

Both had been wishin' that three days of fishin'
Would net them a far bigger catch.
One gold-eye, one whitefish, one perch and one troutfish
Can't win prizes in no fishin' match.

They grumbled and fussed; they spat and they cussed
About their bad luck those three days.
The day after tomorrow they'd be fishin' for oil
Back near Williston, one state away.

"For the time we just lost and the money it cost,
We should've snagged a school or more.
What will we tell folks laughing like hell
When they hear we only caught four?"

"Four chilly nights in this rented camp site
Cost one hundred and sixty bucks.
Plus eighty more to rent them two oars
And a rowboat worth less than corn shucks."

"Two out-of-state permits for this fishin' trip
Dinged us one forty—that's plenty.
I'd say the gas from Williston and back
Comes to another two twenty."

"That's six hundred berries that ain't gifts from fairies
To put just one meal on our dish.
If my arithmetic, shoots straight and quick,
We paid one hundred fifty per fish."

"One hundred fifty dollars," his old pal hollers.
"That skins all I've heard before.
Instead of feelin' down, about the luck we found,
I'm damn glad we didn't catch more."

Six-Shooter Coffee

Crack of Dawn you wake and stir from a bed ground that's half froze.
What starts your cold heart pumping? What thaws out your numb nose?
What's coal black, molasses thick, and four-dollar-pistol hot?
It's the condensed panther poured from the camp cook's coffee pot.

Decades have loped on by since we herded on open range.
But for cow punchers remaining, our coffee taste ain't changed.
We still like it plumb barefoot, no dehorned stuff from town.
No blended stuff from Starbuck's chain. Is Arbuckle still around?

So step up, you short-horns; hear how six-shooter coffee's made.
There ain't no secret to the art; it trailed the cattle trade.
Take a bag of fresh coffee grounds—nothing but Arbuckle brand.
Wet it with some water in a big five-gallon can.

Boil it for the time it takes to tie down a steer or two.
(If you're slow.) Now you're set to test this manly brew.
Now let me tell you how to size up this Arbuckle stew.
Toss your six gun in the can and watch what it'll do.

If your iron sinks, the brew's too weak. Toss more Arbuckle in.
If it floats, your coffee's done. Your roundup can begin.
Your boiler's fired; you're ready to play whatever cards come around.
You damn well wouldn't feel that way drinkin' belly-wash from town.

Mick O'Hara's Zoo

Mick O'Hara was in glee when he found the recipe
To his grandpappy's old Irish brew.
He soaked barley and rye and distilled 'em just right
Till they rotted down to mountain dew.

In his eager haste, he swallowed a taste,
Which led to the next, and then more.
His tonsils were tickled by the fifth trickle,
As he eyed strange critters by the score.

There were elephants pink and he didn't think
The purple snakes were anything but true.
There were reds wolverines and camels bright green
And some unicorns colored sky blue.

Mick was no fool. He almost finished school,
And he knew what a smart hand should do.
He rented a hall, and hung a sign on the wall:
"Come Inside This Amazing Zoo."

"This display features rare exotic creatures,"
The sign rode on to declare.
"You won't see likes of these beasts in your life,
And four bits will cover your fare."

Viewers packed in, waxing sour as sin,
About paying four bits for a look-in.
Empty tables and shelves, and suckers like themselves,
Were the only sights angry eyes took in.

Of course, they shot some words as hot
As a branding iron over the matter.
"If you see purple cats or even grey rats,
O'Hara, you're mad as a hatter."

"What do ya mean, no zoology is seen?
Can't you see these beasts hankering about?
If I was you guys, I'd take my lame eyes
And have a good doc check them out."

Business did boom in that empty room
For a good hour or two.
As you've surmised, a deputy arrived
To shut down Mick O'Hara's zoo.

"This is pure fraud, more low-down than sod.
O'Hara, you're under arrest."
"First have a try at this jig juice, McBride.
To its joyfulness I can attest."

"To duty I've sped. Never let it be said,
That McBride ever drank working shift."
"But this is jig juice the old county cut loose.
One wee nip and your spirits will lift."

"The old country, you say? Well, pass it my way.
Looks just like the juice Daddy brewed.
I guess it won't hurt to down just one squirt,
Certainly not more than two."

One snort of that booze, McBride did choose,
Another, then another, then two.
On the heels of five shots, the Deputy bought
Half interest in O'Hara's Zoo.

Cattle Kate

Ella Watson married a rounder named Harry, when she was but eighteen.
He's unfaithful, at best, so she drifted west, another saloon queen.
She worked eight years as a painted cat near Denver and Cheyenne.
Near Rawlins town she settled down, with a big-time cattle man.

James Averill, 'twas said, owned a huge spread, and made a lot of loot.
Owned a watering hole in town, I'm told, and a grocery store to boot.
Folks branded his mate young Cattle Kate, when with Jim she threw in.
She filed on land, next to his and planned, a life of wicked sin.

Kate traded her favors for mavericks of all flavors, and built up quite a herd.
Jim slapped her brand, on every slick-ear his hands, could steal, was the word.
They worked in the saddle, they hung and rattled, like gameful business
hustlers.
Till other cattle men accused both of them of being cattle rustlers.

In '89, about calving time, vigilantes came for the two.
Kate tried to make an honest break, to avoid what they came to do.
She was chased around, roped, and tied down, and then she and Jim
Were taken in a wagon to a lonely canyon, and lynched with no prayers
or hymns.

A record was set in Wyoming, you bet, on this historic day.
Kate's the only gal Wyoming sent to hell, in this or any other way.

Crude Canadian Geese

As a true-born American son, of our symbol, I'll declare
That no bird on foreign soil to our eagle can compare.
When he soars above the highest peaks, smoother than a hum,
He declares himself ruler of the wilds, for all time to come.

Canada has a majestic bird, the mighty artic goose.
I hear they can cross the sea, and never rest or roost.
Across the big Montana sky, every year in mid spring,
Huge V formations of geese soar to Canada on the wing.

Them northern geese are grand to watch, like a flock of mountain sheep.
Like a herd of buffalo or long horn cattle, it's quite a sight to reap.
But don't expect much etiquette or formality from them flyers.
Their manners are those of a wild critter, unsettled as prairie fires.

Now when they make their spring crusade, some dung they must release.
They don't seek an outhouse or public latrine; they unload where they please.
They don't seem to give a hoot if it's town or country below.
Be hill or dale, farm or ranch, when they have to go, they go.

My Pa in Law one spring day was plowin' in his Poppin' John.
He cut the engine to sit and listen to a formation honking its song.
Seems one big honker couldn't wait till the big V passed our spread.
He dropped his load; we watched it splatter, on top of Pop's bald head.

My Ma in Law saw the mishap, and she came dashing down
With a roll of tissue in her hand to wipe his messy crown.
As she pranced up, he said, "Too late for toilet paper, Dear.
By now it's plain as plowed ground, he's a good two miles from here."

Airing Out the Lungs

"When it comes to cussing, don't swallow your tongue.
Use both barrels, and air out your lungs."
  An old-time cowboy proverb.

There are certain words common to buffalo skinners
And men who hit their thumbs with a hammer,
Not fit for your church's pot luck dinners
Or to write on a Sunday school banner.
Language that could melt all the frost
Out of a November zero morning.
Make the words a stuck bullwhacker tossed
Sound like a sermon, dry and boring.

Language to scorch the atmosphere
And burn a few acres of grass.
Language no lady should have to hear,
Or any corn-fed, prim, sweet lass.
Language that makes the air turn blue,
Words hot enough to sizzle bacon.
Old-time profanity, tried and true,
To accompany commandment breakin'.

Most cowboys could cuss handy as the rest,
Sounding like a mule skinners' convention.
When we burned the ground, we met the test,
But blasphemy was never our intention.
This cowboy never cussed to commit
Sin against the Lord, not me.
There's a heap of difference, you must admit,
Between cowboy cussing and blasphemy.

When a cowboy horned a critter or a man
With his double barrel syllables,
It's not for wish to be wicked, understand.
It's from habit, this vocabulary he unfolds.
It's a rider's way of blowing off steam
When his patience dries and withers.
Cussin' won't help to keep the soul clean,
But it sure takes some strain off the liver.

But a top hand at airing out his lungs
Don't want to blasphemize one minute.
It's a natural part of his native tongue.
He crams plenty of grammar in it.
But he never cussed without a cause,
Like many a cussin' modern fool.
Cussin' showed the livestock who was boss,
The only lingo understood by a mule.

Sometimes a string of sizzling sounds
That could blister the toughest hide
Were in the spirit of pals horsing abound
When expressed on the lighter side.
If the verbage was cast out with a smile
And in tones of frivolity,
It was taken as a joke for a while
With an air of chivalry.

But if these flaming words were spoke
In tones frosty as a December night,
A cow puncher knew it was no joke.
It was time to dismount and fight.
There was an art to cussin', a cowboy learns,
It was inventive, too.
He didn't use a few worn-out terms
Like modern city cussers do.

Each rider hatched up his own vocab
Of phrases and lines he'd invent.
It was a spoken language we had.
It didn't look good in print.
Each cow hand had his private cavvy
Of his invented vulgar lines.
All cowboys who were copy-right savvy
Didn't infringe on his wording so fine.

But if a lady was within his sight,
He'd let no hot words stray.
He cinched the lid on his cuss words tight
To cut loose another day.

When Lucky Joined the Tribe

We were bellied up in the Mint Saloon
After the bull ridin' played out,
Crookin' our elbows to every rider in the room,
Perched painting their noses throughout.

Then in blows a rounder we'd taken for dead.
Hadn't seen him in two years or three.
"It's me, Lucky," was the first thing he said.
"That's how you can still address me.

"But soon I'll be heap chief of the Blackfeet,
Leading that great Indian nation
Higher up the totem pole of esteem
Than any prior western sensation.

"The Blackfeet elders made me their son;
Took me into their tribe of great fame.
I think it means you're a tribal one
When they hang on you a native name.

"Today I'm just a low-totem-pole brave
Sporting a new Blackfoot name.
It's a name I'll cherish till I'm in the grave,
But old pals, call me Lucky, just the same.

"I plan to shine in the ridin' and ropin'
In all them Indian rodeos.
And soon I'll be known as the only brave lopin'
Who couldn't be outscored or throwed.

"And then my new name will fall on the ears
Of every bold Blackfoot around.
I'll rise to be chief and bring back the years
Of tribal pride, power, and renown."

"Buffalo chips! How can that be true?"
A rider roped at him to tell.
"How can a drifter as lazy as you
Impress the wise Blackfeet so well?"

"This past Friday eve I sauntered in,
To a big open Blackfoot powwow.
I danced them inter-tribals time and again
Without nobody showin' me how.

"I kicked up the dust and hoofed the hard ground
Like a rampaging, wild range cow.
When the sun rose, and the drums ceased to pound,
I stopped dancing and took a deep bow.

"It was then, pards, my new Blackfoot name
Was hung onto me by the chiefs.
Saying, 'You must come back and dance again
With us some day, Clumsy Feet.'"

Braggers and Bitchers

As I remarked prior, motion picture shows,
Dime novels and TV, after the radios,
Painted crooked pictures of the row a cowboy hoes,
On a pedestal as we kneel at his feet.

Made us think his shootin' hand's lightning fast,
He's a wall of courage no outlaw got passed,
Who could throw and tie a slick with each loop he cast,
And he boasted like this about each feat:

...I can make a fuzzy lariat whistle wild and whirl
And win the heart of almost any prairie girl.
I can throw the toughest critter that ever grew a horn.
In a rockin' covered wagon, that's where I was born.
I'm a rootin', tootin' cowboy, my guns tight at my hip.
Many a man has bit the dust because he made a slip.
I suppose you think I'm braggin, but I can ride some too.
And every word I say to you, I swear by gum is true... *

If said oratory weren't enough to win a cowboy's spurs,
There's more vivid boasts, he lernt while trailing herds:

"I can ride a streak of lightning across the northern skies.
Once I rode a black tornado for seven hundred miles.
I can rope a thousand steers and leave 'em tied in piles.
And I've roped and tied down a cyclone or two.

"I broke a twelve-foot gator across my bended knee.
I hugged a full grown grizzly until he pleaded for mercy.
I whipped my weight in bobcats one day they troubled me.
I'd tote a steamboat across the Missouri for you."

If them boasts still weren't enough to fool one and all,
There's even more manly bluffs upon which he could call:

"I was suckled by a she bear and I rode a mountain lion.
I ate prickly pear and picked my teeth with a .44 iron.
I eat snakes and crocodiles; I'll eat the man who says I'm lyin'.
I drink blood and eat tarantulas to lose weight.

"One squint from my eye once blistered a bull's hide.
The flash of my glance killed an oak tree, tall and white.
I've got the toughest stallion and the ugliest dog in sight.
If it ain't true, cut me up for catfish bait."

There's a heap of difference between what your books spell,
What your taking boxes say and what your movies tell,
And the true cowboy life—oh, I knew it well.
So the naked truth, I'll wade in and unfold:

A cow hand whose bragging shot well over par
Could boast himself out of friends, near and afar,
And a place to stand and lean his elbows on the bar.
These ain't buffalo chips or corral dust I unload.

Some men are all gurgle, but they have no guts.
They often throw up more than their share of corral dust.
Such fools seem to think the sun comes up just
To listen to the loud braggers crow.

Some young waddies get calluses, in fact,
From patting themselves too much on the back.
But deeds to back up their words they lack,
And words can never make a coward bold.

A man who wants to show too much spread
Is bound to get his horns clipped instead.
We didn't cotton to braggers, alive or dead,
In the true Western days bold and old.

But there's one man even less welcome, I swear,
Than the jack mule who brays every where
About the Lord giving him more than his share.
It's the cowboy who bellows like a steer.

He'll pitch on his rope, howling like a tied coon,
Arching his back while he whines a sour tune,
And raise a war yell they can hear on the moon,
Slamming complaints at every one near.

But kicking never gets a man any where,
Unless you're a mule; then you shouldn't care.
A kicking mule can't pull a wagon here or there,
And a pulling mule sure can't ever kick.

Never complain; it makes you welcome as a skunk,
As a wet dog in a parlor or a snake in a bunk,
As a turd in your boot or a whore to a monk.
So don't you dare turn that bitcher's trick.

* The lyrics in italics are from the late Wilf Carter's song, "Sundown Slim."
Carter, a Canadian, was known in the U.S. as "Montana Slim."

Red Tape

I'm as patriotic as a rancher can get.
Vote, pay taxes, bet your hat I'm a vet.
So why do our governments—federal, county, state—
Tie this cowboy down with lariats of red tape?

My herd of cattle is pint-sized at best,
On ground that can scarce feed a rabbit.
So I barkeep in a watering hole, the Crow's Nest
To support my cattle-raisin' habit.

Monday my fattest steer fetched loose
And strayed on the Great Northern Line.
Every wheel of a fast freight from engine to caboose
Made ground round of that cow of mine.

I called the dispatcher from a pay phone out back
Saying, "Sorry for the blood on your train.
No need for a rep to go clear the track.
What's left will wash away come first rain."

He called the sheriff, who called Uncle Sam
Because the railroad runs interstate.
He called the state capitol and some insurance man,
Who said, "You'll pay, cowboy; just wait."

Then came a passel of questions on forms
From bureaucrats everywhere but here,
Asking long questions in four-legged words
About the ups and downs of that steer.

Its name, occupation, birthday and weight;
The size of his feet, horns, and tail.
His mother's maiden name and her wedding date,
And how many miles he'd trailed.

How high was that pile of forms, do you ask?
My answer could make a man quiver.
It was higher than the Anaconda smokestack
And twice as long as the Sun River.

I filled out forms from dawn till midnight.
At the turn, the last question appeared.
One I couldn't answer, very quick and right,
Read, "Disposition of the dead steer?"

I could've told them the outlaw's brand
Or the number of rings on his horns.
But all I could write about disposition, off hand,
Was, "He seemed calm, peaceful, and bored."

Hooch

It ain't that I never down a drink.
Please don't get me wrong.
I wouldn't want you folks to think
In the tea-totalers pile I belong.

I like a beer or a shot or two
Like most any cattle man.
But downing more than just a few
Is no longer in my hand.

I'm through surrounding a lion's share
And getting toilet-huggin' drunk.
No more chugaluggin' on a dare.
Like I did as a wild young buck.

I used to belly up to the bar,
My sorrows all to drown.
I irrigated them all the more
Each time I rode to town.

It don't take much backbone
To belly up to a bar.
If it takes hooch your courage to hone,
You've played that card too far.

No corkscrew's ever known to lift
A troubled man out of a hole.
Too much of Dionysus' gift
Leaves ya tipsy and melts your roll.

The stuff that makes you tipsy soon
Will make you tip your hand,
Making it plain to all in the room
You ain't no thinking man.

When you leave with nothing but a head,
You'd better take a second look.
It means your brain cavity—feeling like lead—
Is empty as your pocket book.

The man who tries to conserve boot soles
By keeping them on a brass rail
Always has too small a roll
To buy new boots for the trail.

Giving liquor to certain folks
Is like playing harp with a hammer.
Saddled with a mood that can't take jokes,
Toward trouble they tend to clammer.

Hunting trouble in saloons, I fear,
You're bound to cash in your chips
Face down with sawdust in your beard,
Blood oozing from between your lips.

So when you down a shot or two,
Don't take another bottle home.
Charlie Russell said, "Enjoy good brew,
But it's bad medicine drinking alone."

To leave you with a worthy tip,
This advice I hereby render:
One smile from a good woman's lips
Beats a hundred from a bartender.

A Tombstone for Sale

One thing always makes me fret
About my wife and daughter.
They hold onto money like
A fishing net holds water.

I'm no top hand at bragging,
But I can boastfully say,
I have the first buck I ever earned.
I earned it just today.

I've been rode for never holding a job
To support my poor family.
But I found a job with hundreds—
No thousands—of people under me.

It's what ya call a sit-down job.
The work ain't never hard.
I drive a little tractor/mower
Cutting grass in the grave yard.

I stop to read the writing on
The tombstones of life's winners.
Them pious words all make me wonder,
"Where do they bury the sinners?"

One gravestone boasts, "I still live."
For a corpse, that ain't quite fit.
I may not always tell the truth,
But when I'm dead, I'll own up to it.

"Here lies a lawyer and an honest man,"
Another stone reads of kin.
Who'd ever guess two manly corpses
Could fit in a hole that thin?

So if you need a granite stone
I can deal you a used one.
It's truly a bargain if your name
Just happens to be Olson.

Jingle In The Pockets

"A cowboy goes to town and spends his money 'round,
Whenever he gets that jingle in his jeans.
He'll never learn to save; he's gonna squander till his grave,
Whenever he gets that jingle in his jeans.
When that jingle starts to jangle, he'll dance like a Bojangle,
Buy the rounds and wind up feeling just a little bit mean—in the morning.
I always go to town and spend my money 'round,
*Whenever I get that jingle in my jeans..." ***

Like most cowboys, this ruttin' buck
Paid tomorrow too little heed.
On pay day my old Chevy truck
Would rush me to damn fool deeds.

When I got jingle in my jeans,
It melted like mist in the sun
On thievin', cheatin' poker machines,
Shots of whiskey, brandy and fun.

I hung on to money back then
Like a net hangs on to water.
The last of my jingle always went
To some rancher's two-steppin' daughter.

My roll played out, this staggering stud
Somehow made it home to bed.
I'd wake with a drum of sour blood
Still throbbing in my head.

Then a filly cut my trail one day,
And in her love loop I was caught.
Soon every splinter of my pay
Went for this farm we bought.

Men grow up and face some tests
From this world as hard as rock.
Like a drunk, the tighter money gets,
The louder it seems to talk.

Here's my steer—and don't knock it—
I've learned after thirty crops.
The biggest hole in a man's pocket
Is the one that's at the top.

Money that burns hot like a rocket
Is shooting for a fiery crash.
The man whose money burns his pocket
Never has any cold, hard cash.

Once our farm could finally make
Some cash to save and spend,
Too many guys asked, "Can you stake
Me to a loan, old friend?"

I'm always sad to have to deny
An old pal making a touch.
But sometimes tying to stake a guy
Don't improve things all that much.

There are folks you'd like to trust
Who burn a month's pay on a spree.
Often their state of owing you dust
Causes loss of their memory.

Sometimes you may share their sorrow
And caper to their yearnings,
To find they think what they borrow
Is just part of their earnings.

The buck they borrow ain't half the size
Of the greenback dollar you lend.
It's common as gophers to see these guys
Borrow themselves out of a friend.

It's cheaper to give money than to lend
To a man gone broke from fun.
By playing that card, you make a friend,
'stead of always losing one.

So let me unload this grass-root
Steer my grampa endorsed:
It's wisest to just go on foot
Till you can afford a horse.

* The italicized song lyrics are from Sean Blackburn's western swing
song, "Jingle in My Jeans," recorded with Liz Masterson in 1991.

A Cool Stud

Down a washboard road, with a two-ton load, of chopped hay three cowhands sped.
It was their fate, on this cruel date, they'd be pronounced quite dead.
The pickup didn't crash; its roof wasn't bashed, in from huge falling rocks.
They cashed in their chips from of a waddy named Rip and the medicine in his pill box.

Rip turned the latch that opened the hatch of that pill box of shiny tin.
He unscrewed a lid and down his gullet slid a fistful of vitamins.
His liver pills followed the pain pills he swallowed; then came his anti-histamine,
Bacteria pills, depression pills, heart pills and strong Benzedrine.

A pill for digestion, a pill for congestion, and something called Bromo Quinine,
A tranquilizing pill and a stay-awake pill he chased with two shots of Listerine.
He unloaded a joke and then rolled a smoke, in spite of the truck's bumpy motion.
To light a stick match, he gave his boot a scratch, then Lord, what an awful explosion!

As they winged their way to St. Peter that day, he headed them off at the gate.
He sighed with a frown, "Our computers are down; you cowboys will just have to wait.
We can't take you in till they boot up again, so here's what you'll have to do.
Return to your lives, your friends and your wives, till we send an angel for you."

"We'd love to, dear Saint, but we're sure there ain't, no way that trick can be turned.
An explosion from Hell left every dang cell in our bodies all scattered and burned."
"I guess that's true. So what shall we do?" said St. Peter of the bad news.
"I know, my friends. Go back again, as any of God's creatures you choose."

Said one, "Sir, I gather, there's nothing I'd rather, do on this day I must die,
Than an eagle be, so bold and so free, soaring through my kingdom, the sky."
"If that be your will, then let us fulfill, this wish you have harbored so long."
The Saint kindly smiled, then prayed a short while, and the eagle wannabe was gone.

The second man said, "If I must be dead, I can't pass an adventure so rare.
Kind Saint, before I rest, make me King of the West, the mighty ruling grizzly bear."
"If that be your will, then let us fulfill, this wish you have harbored so long."
The Saint kindly smiled, then prayed a short while, and the grizzly wannabe was gone.

The third deceased, who spoke his short peace, was Rip, who swallowed the pills.
He said, "Kind Sir, I think I'm quite sure, what I'll wish for my final thrills.
I've always been lonely; I looked strange and homely, and never could rope up a wife.
The fillies I roped at, called me ugly and fat, saying I'd be a nerd all my life.

"Just once can I try being a cool guy, instead of a lost social dud?
When you send me back, please put me on track, of existing as a cool stud."
"If that be your will, then let us fulfill, this wish you have harbored so long."
The Saint kindly smiled, then prayed a short while, and the cool stud wannabe was gone.

Four hours passed; St. Peter at last, called an angel to his holy gate.
"Tell those three men we're booted up again; I hope they enjoyed the nice wait."
"Sir, do you know, where I must go, to find the one with talons and beak?"
"Yes," the Saint smiled, "He's soaring a mile above Colorado's top peak."

"And where shall I sail to pick up the trail of the one you turned into a bear?"
"Fly like a lark to the heights of Glacier Park; you'll find that kingly beast there."
"And that social dud who emerged a cool stud; where in creation is he?"
"'Twas a strange request, but I did my best. He's on a snow tire near Calgary."

Range Calico

Grampa said that in his hay day, pretty range calico
Was scarce as clean socks in a bunkhouse, or a two-legged buffalo.
"I'd trot twenty miles on a Saturday eve, banking on the chance
There'd be loose fillies shakin' their hooves, at the grange hall dance.
But when the band was all tuned up and ready for the fun,
The steers always outnumbered the heifers, a good twenty to one.

"The few she-folk that cowhands ever saw sauntering around
Came by steamship, when the river was high, to Fort Benton town.
Them calico heifers had their pick of all manner of men.
None came hankering to wed us cowhands way back then.
Some picked merchants, some found doctors, bankers, or legal charmers.
Some picked men who owned a mine, a big ranch, or funeral
embalmers.

"But I never held a higher hand than a pair of threes and a deuce
Whenever the stakes were a spry young filly, or a widow on the loose.
Without money to throw to the birds, you don't hold openers.
You draw a four spot to a queen, and your losing hand never betters.
A cowboy, after running with a straight steer herd so long,
Was shy as a young prairie dog, or a new-foiled bronc.

"Let me chip in a strange fact I've come to know so well.
It's easier to face a gun than the face of a pretty gal.
The glance of a pretty gal's eye, when it's flashed toward me,
Can be more terrifying than the glimmer of a sharp bowie.
There's nothing on the western range like a specimen of she-stuff
To make a cowhand lose the trail and get his spurs tangled up.

"Oh, in my prime I tossed my verbal lariat at a few,
Just trying to find out what the stray fillies would do.
Would she sunfish, pitch or buck, or try to run on the rope?
Or would she prove to be halter broke, like I'd always hope?
But every time I cast my tie at a heifer who had strayed,
My loop would fail to open or some brush was in the way.

"I'd go to church, thinking it's the place to meet a wife,
Allowin' it was time for me to settle down for life.
I'd try my best, after hearing the preacher's holy word,
To cut a pretty range heifer out of that gospel herd.
But before I could ever snag a pretty piece of gingham,
She'd be roped and tied down by a man who owned half a kingdom.

"The only hope I had to ever marry, I did decide,
Was to try to rope onto a mail-order bride.
I sent the matrimonial outfit my picture one spring morn.
If I hadn't played that card, you grandkids wouldn't be born.
They said my bride-to-be would arrive within at best twelve days,
An eastern gal who graded corn-fed, too good to run with the strays.

"My single-footer cowboy pals, who I knew from the trail,
Warned me marriage is risky as braiding a mule's tail.
'When a cowboy throws in with a wife, love and lives to share,
It's sorta like eating off the same plate with a mama bear.
Whenever a woman on the wed starts in draggin' her rope,
Why's there always a fool willing to step into her loop?

"'You can't turn a woman's mind when it's in stampede,
No more than a runaway hog or a wild band of steeds.
It's easier to hold five hundred horses on a thundering night
Than to ride herd on the heart of one lady, wrong or right.
They're surely ranging cattle, and they're always on the move.
You can bet on horses, cards, or fights, but never bet on love.

"'A man caught in a woman's loop is a bear cub without paws.
He's helpless as a dummy with his hands and feet cut off.
When her wits are in stampede, and her fatal course is chose,
You can't check her with a three-quarters rope and snubbing post.
The reason God created woman last, you must understand,
Is 'cause He didn't want no criticism while creating man.'

"For eleven days I heard them, slinging warnings to and fro.
On the twelfth I hitched the buggy and to the depot I rode.
She looked a little like her picture—maybe a tad older,
And maybe just a touch more plump, but not enough to scold her.
Although she didn't trail in pretty as a diamond flush,
I'm no parlor ornament either; I couldn't kick too much.

"But more important, I'll chip in this, and back my play with money,
She was full of sweetness as a bee tree's full of honey.
She was as fine a lady as ever flipped a flapjack.
I couldn't part with her for forty cows; bet your spurs on that.
A woman's heart's like a camp fire; take my steer; don't refuse it.
You must tend to it regular, or sure enough, you'll lose it.

"She was mother of all flowers, a daisy dipped in dew.
In spite of her heart's tenderness, she was tough as rawhide too.
Them early Montana range brides were as hardy as their men.
They had to be, to take the work and weather way back then.
If a Montana stockman ever amounted to a pinch of snuff,
It was 'cause his wife stood with him when life was so tough."

Too many things in life have changed out on the windy range,
But the scarcity of calico on the Highline's still unchanged.
But there's still matrimonial outfits dealing the catalog game.
Their aim is still to see gents wed, but the layout ain't the same.
They send a fellow to meet the bride, in some far off land.
Modern girls are too soft and spoilt for a cattle hand.

Grampa said, "If you take a mind to rope up a catalog bride,
Soak in these words I spill and by these words abide.
You won't understand her tongue; she likely won't savvy yours.
So invent a lingo with your hands, words that never curse.
And learn to talk with your face and eyes; youngsters, I'll tell you,
Sometimes they say more than words, and always shoot more true.

"The worst women ever born are better than the best men.
So always treat her with respect and love her till the end.
And stuff these words in your Stetson for all posterity:
If you don't treat her like the bell mare she must be,
I hope she pulls her picket pin and drifts to unclaimed range
And hitches to a deserving gent who loves her for a change."

Sorrow in a Small Town Church

As he'd done forty years, dear Brother O'Lear, grasped the rope to the steeple bell.
Just like his granddad and great granddad had, he helped save us sinners from hell.
To remind all with chime it was worship time, was his duty each Sunday morn.
After forty years, and four litters of O'Lears, it seemed that's why he was born.

He took a firm hold and heartily pulled on the hemp rope his great granddad wound.
Anxious to bring the bell's merry ring, but the rope snapped like straw and fell down.
He feared the bell's chime wouldn't toll this one time, the first time in its history.
After four generations, this sad situation shouldn't come to haunt his family.

"I can't let this be. It's all up to me, to find a way to ring that bell.
Before I start ditchin' my family tradition, I'd roast in the fires of hell."
A ladder he found that was laying around in back of the cathedral's shed.
The ladder seemed strong, but not very long, four feet short of the roof's edge.

Feet on the top rung, his left hand hung to the mount that anchored the bell.
And with his free right he pushed for all might, hearing those sweet bell chimes swell.
Out with a DING and back with a DONG, the ringing tolled through the place.
His hand missed a DONG and with a loud BONG, the bell clubbed him in the face.

A rearward lurch bucked him off his perch; speeding toward the ground he came,
With twists and dips and fancy back flips that put Olympic divers to shame.
The corpse on the ground brought a small herd around, and two police in their attire.
"Did you see or hear what transpired here?" the cops to bystanders inquired.

They all shook their heads and everyone said they were sorry to miss the crash landing.
But it's plain to tell the deceased party fell from the belfry above where we're standing.
"Do you know his name? Or from where he came? Or perhaps what wares does he sell?"
One said, "I can't claim to know the man's name, but his face sure does ring a bell."

O'Lear had a brother, from the same dad and mother, younger by a year or two.
I'll swear each brother did favor the other, like two bottles of the same brew.
Brother Martin declared he'd do his share to make his ancestors proud.
He swore right away that every Sunday, he'd sound that bell clear and loud.

Time came to ascend to the stairway's end, and pull that rope to beat the band.
But to his consternation, the whole congregation had forgot to replace the bell's strand.
"Two centuries of, my family's love, ain't gonna bog down today.
I'll ring the darn bell, or send me to hell. Satan, get out of my way."

He weaseled his way out the window and placed a foot on the fixture's narrow ledge,
Till all ten fingers clamped to the shingles of the roof's splintery edge.
With the last of his power, he cooned up the tower, feeling his heart loudly pounding,
Found a place to stand, and with one free hand, he set that old bell to sounding.

Out with a DING and back with a DONG, he pushed the bell with family pride.
Before it could fade, he overplayed, and slid down the roof's other side.
He bounced off the edge, just missed a hedge, and soaring to the ground he came
In a perfect swan dive. I'd bet my last five, he put Olympic divers to shame.

The crowd was the same, the same police came, asking, "Now who fell from the tower?
We need to know where the deceased must go; he'll be stiff as slate in an hour."
One said, "I don't know where lived the poor soul, or even the name that you seek.
But I'm a humdinger if he ain't a dread ringer, for that guy who cashed in last week."

Saddle Blanket Gamblers

"You can tell a good saddle blanket gambler by the rig he's settin' in."

"It don't take long for a gambling cowhand to get his money into circulation."
   Two old-time cowboy proverbs.

Most cattle outfits outlawed cards; games caused loss of sleep.
They caused some losers to chew manes and long grudges to keep.
But the range bosses couldn't ride herd on saddle-blanket games.
Broker than the Ten Commandments, we played stud all the same.

Using beans for poker chips, we played draw by the fire.
But the joy was sometimes dampened, when the stakes grew higher.
Many a fine saddle switched brands from fools over-bettin'.
You could tell a good gambler by the rig on which he's settin'.

On pay day we'd hit the saloons after weeks of pushing hides.
The saloons hit back with the right bait to keep us fools inside:
Snakewater, blackjack, monte, faro, five-card draw and stud,
Waiting to lift a cowboy's roll and leave him poor as mud.

Against a thoroughbred card sharp, who played the odds and reasoned,
Saddle blanket gamblers had less show than stub-tail bulls in fly season.
A cowhand's roll didn't last as long as his half pint of Redeye.
"Play 'em high and sleep in the streets," well sums up every try.

Some dealers seemed to know, somehow, both sides of every card.
Such dealers could out-hold, somehow, a warehouse or stock yard.
A friendly game might start off slow, but then it gathers moss,
Till your roll, your saddle, your gun and spurs, sure as sin are lost.

Outlawing people's vices never gets shed of them much.
Poker moved into back rooms, cellars, barns and such.
The stakes grew higher than King's Hill; crooked as a posthole auger.
Even the antes grew too high for a cowboy, farmer, or logger.

Sixty years after outlawing poker, it's back in most watering holes.
But now men gamble against machines, built to skin your rolls.
They'll let you win a hand or two, to keep you in the game,
But when your spree is all played out, you're poorer than you came.

It's easier to embark on a game with machines, I'm told.
No need to round up other sharps, or enter a game cold.
Robot sharps may peel your roll slower than dealers do,
But they sure corral all the chips of fools like me and you.

You get addicted to 'em, too, the mental sharps keep warning.
They say it's harder to quit that vice, than to quit your snoring.
I still play cards a little, but I'll tell you on the level.
I'd no more place bets on machines than cut for deal with the devil.

Both the devil and machines hide aces, their evil hands to fill.
They always slip cards from the bottom and skin you at their will.
So I'll cut the deck with old cattlemen, and learn to understand
How to know from their faces and eyes, what cards are in their hand.

The Winning Team

We crossed the cattle guard, me and my pard, and rode up the trail to
the creek,
Prowlin' for strays in the mid morning haze, who missed being branded
last week.
Riding northwest, we did our best, to spook them steers from the draws.
But an antelope, a crow, a jackrabbit and a doe, were the only critters we saw.

We met on our mission two NoDaks fishin'. We waved 'em hello from
the saddle.
Without sliding down to the chilly damp ground, we asked if they'd seen
any cattle.
A radio layin' near the bank was playin', a stirring announcer of fame.
'Twas top of the eighth, and we couldn't wait, to know who's winning
the game.

My friend Waddy yells, loud as church bells, to the NoDaks fishin' the
banks.
"We won't ask any more if you tell us the score. We bet a tall stack on
the Yanks."
"It's ten to eight; one just crossed the plate; they've scored runs most
every inning."
"Thank you, my pal, but you didn't tell, my pardner and me who was
winning."

They stared at each other for a spell, then another, blank as they looked
while fishin'.
A confab they held, and us riders could tell, they'd come to no hasty
decision.
I heard the crowd roar. "Did somebody score?" "No, the score's still eight
to ten."
"And who'd you say was ahead, anyway?" They both proudly grinned
and said, "Ten."

Country and Western
Songs for the New West

We grew up strong, and tough as tacks, on that windy Montana range,
When country was country, men were men, and women were men just
the same.
We heard the songs about working cattle, about love and low-down cheaters.
The most high tech things in our homes were manual egg beaters.

But the years brought on a passel of changes we can't yet conceive,
Enough to make an old cow hand want to saddle up and leave.
To the range came foreign livestock that nobody here had seen,
Critters like llamas and alpacas, and ostriches, tall and lean.

People came to the Big Sky Country from all across the nation.
People steeped in suburban ways with computerized occupations.
Realtors, councilors, investors, and tourist trappers flocked in,
Sportin' politically correct words and hides that are too thin.

Today all the old country songs don't fit the land no more:
About herding cattle in the saddle until your rump felt sore.
Songs of loving, songs of fighting, songs of untamed lands,
Songs of mother, songs of freedom, of prison and outlaw bands.

Songs of work and songs of play, songs of getting drunk.
Songs of praise and lazy days and barnyards full of junk.
Songs of trains and bridle reins, songs of friends and kin.
Songs of dancing in honkytonks, and songs of forgiving sin.

The songs we heard our radios and bands play with a twang,
The songs we loved to remember in the bunkhouse where we sang,
Don't seem to fit the land today, though they were once the best.
So we rounded up a new Hit Parade of songs for the New West.

Number twenty-four on the hit parade, formerly number three,
From a movie about subdivided estates, "They Call the Wind Tiffany."
New this week at twenty-three, and climbing up the charts,
Is Hank the fourth with his new hit, "Your Disingenius Heart."

Hit number twenty-two is by a Texan named John-Glen.
It's brand new to the charts this week, "I'm Back in the Volvo Again."
Holding fast, same as last week, at number twenty-one,
Is Ernie Chevy's new hit single, "Sixteen Metric Tons."

Cowboy Copus is back again, although his voice has changed.
Singing number twenty called, "My Disfunctional Home on the Range."
Hit number nineteen this week should top out by and by.
Rising quickly up the charts is "Ghost R-Vers in the Sky."

Down from number twenty-four, starting to decline,
Is number eighteen, "Ruby, Don't Take Your Love on Line."
Willie sings number seventeen, his first new hit this year,
Called, "Blue Chips, Growth Stocks, and Micro Brewed Beer."

Number sixteen is by a new-comer; perhaps by now you've bought it.
It's Montana Fats' first big single, "I'm Heading for the Final Audit."
Number fifteen is a rewrite of a politically incorrect version,
Down from number seventeen, called, "Stand By Your Person."

Number Fourteen's climbing fast, a chart buster to come,
Bound to be on top soon, "Take These Stock Options and Shove 'Em."
Merle is back with his patriotic songs of being free.
Here's hit thirteen, "You're Walking on the Litigating Side of Me."

Number twelve's a brand new hit, growing hotter and hotter.
Sung by the Sons of the Country Club, called, "Cool Bottled Water."
Now that Johnny Cash is gone, who will fill his shoes?
Johnny Credit Card has hit eleven, "Folsom Correctional Facility Blues."

Number ten is by Mr. Rogers, his second hit, back to back,
Aptly called, "Drifting Along with the Tumbling Plastic Sacks."
Number nine this week is by the Judd girl and her mother.
Climbing fast is "I Want To Be A Cowboy's Significant Other."

Number eight is a favorite of folks who don't want rap or rock.
Remade from an old Gene Autry hit, "You Are My Sun Block."
Number seven is rising fast, sung by Sure-foot Dan.
Trucking songs ain't in no more. Here's "S.U.V. Driving Man."

Hit number six is up from slot eleven since last week.
"Don't Let Your Babies Grow Up To Be Realtors," bound to hit the peak.
Number five is up four notches; its success is more than lucky.
Sung by Merle is "I'm Proud to be a Yuppie from Kentucky."

Hank Junior recorded number four to repay the government.
"All My Rowdy Friends Have Taken Early Retirement."
Holding steady at number three is by new-comer Sam Hall.
His first big hit, surely not his last, is "The Lonesome Llama Call."

Number two's down from number one, a song taken from a poem.
Porter Corvette sings this one, "The Xeriscaped Grass of Home."
That takes us up to number one; a song well worth the wait.
"Help Me Make It Through The Night, Viagra," up from number eight.

Ride easy, and save the best of your mount for the end of the trail.
Don't get knots in your lariat, and don't get your spurs tangled up.